PRAISE FOR *PROFIT F*

So often in dental school, we don't get eno
practices—never mind the financial piece.
dentists and know how critically importan
putting a system in place to support your financial goals. *Profit First for Dentists* does just that. It should be required reading for all dental students as they exit into their new careers.

>Dr. MaryJane Hanlon, Associate Dean of Clinical Affairs, Tufts University School of Dental Medicine, and founder of The New Dentist Symposium and The Women in Dentistry Podcast

Profit First for Dentists is a must-read for anyone in private practice dentistry! The simple concept of paying yourself first works in other areas of our finances, but why don't we put it into place in our practices? See, this simple concept of taking my profit first and then being given the step-by-step approach to make it happen has made me truly excited to accomplish something I've only thought about for a long time but never consistently achieved: make my business profitable! Thank you, Barb and Drew!

>Scott Price, DMD, East Valley Periodontics, Mesa, AZ

Barb Stackhouse has spent her career helping dentists succeed, first as a periodontal co-therapist in practice, then as a consultant, coach, and mentor to dentists and their teams. She has seen firsthand that success in dentistry does not assure success in business, something that most dental professionals are not made aware of in their training. This book will guide you through a proven method, one which Barb has made specific to dentistry, to build your business success so that you can reach your full potential as a dentist and give your best to the people you went into dentistry to serve. Do not be surprised by its simplicity, for that is its power, a power to change your mindset and your behaviors.

>Gary DeWood, DDS, MS, Executive Vice President, Spear Education

I wish I had this book ten years ago. It was then that I met Barb, who was a hygienist and coach at a teaching center I was attending. I learned about overhead control, business principles, and saving money. Yet it all seemed so complicated, and was time-consuming. Fast forward to 2021, and Barb has taken what used to be a complicated process, combined it with Profit First ideals, and streamlined it to fit the dental profession. After reading this book, I have decided to put the "old ways" aside, adopt Barbara's teachings to place Profit First in my practice, and look forward to many years of profits.

>Carl Futenma, DDS, Creative Smiles, Vancouver, WA

Certain that I was about to see the end of my dental business, I reached out to an old friend. Barb Stackhouse and I met years ago while she was in Arizona and solidified our friendship when the AGD held its annual meeting in Nashville, TN. Other practice management systems cannot produce the results possible with Profit First. That bold statement is evidenced by the current state of my practice. Two years after what I was sure was the demise of my practice, the Profit First system ensured that I was positioned to survive a complete shutdown from mid-March until early June, and a limited (50%) re-opening until the third week of August, 2020. My team was fully compensated while no income was realized for over ten weeks. We are stronger today than when we closed in March! Barb fluently translates the language of Profit First into words all dentists can comprehend. The best solution is always the simple one, and this system is proof. Read the book, do the work, and enjoy the fruits of your labor.

Nicholas F. Gardner, DDS, Gouverneur, NY

I have to start by saying that Barb and Drew hit an absolute home run! Or, in dentistry terms, cut the most beautiful prep, took the most impeccable impression, or just completed the most spectacular full-mouth rejuvenation of a lifetime. The authors' ability to tell the truth about what is quite often the demise of the dental practice is sobering and, at the same time, brings such hope to all dentists. The simple step-by-step strategy of Profit First gives anyone the power to instantly start turning the boat around. This is an absolute must-read for any dentist who dreams of living the life they deserve. Thank you for elevating this wonderful profession!

Daniel J. O'Rourke, CEO, Dentistry's Optimal Model, Bozeman, MT

Drew Hinrichs is a CPA and tax strategist, and Barb Stackhouse is a hygienist and dental practice business coach; they are both Profit First Professionals. In this book, they lay out a clear plan that flips the above equation: Sales – Profit = Expenses. Pay yourself first. I know that if you are a dentist, like I am, this seems impossible!

I have had the opportunity to not only review this book but listen to one of the authors, Barbara Stackhouse, in person. She has been a mentor of mine for over twenty years. She has coached dentists one-on-one and practices this Profit distribution herself. If you are a dentist, the owner of a dental practice, or an associate dentist, this book is for you!

Lindsay Goss, DMD, MPH, Mesa, AZ

Someone has finally translated a successful business self-help book to dentistry! With Mike Michalowicz's support, Barb Stackhouse applied his Profit First system to the dental practice budget. As an experienced practice coach for dentists, she quickly connects readers with common problems and pressures of ownership (including debt), then walks through the process step by step, directly relating the applications to successful current clients. Barb spells out how to set realistic goals, shares common traps people fall into when implementing this process, and emphasizes the importance of sequence. She knows how dentists think, and keeps them from jumping to the bottom line with this easy read for the busy professional. The book has links to online tools and supports those who go live on their own.

Whether you are a practice owner struggling to make ends meet or someone who thinks you have this figured out, reading this book can increase your profits exponentially.

Ron Albert, DMD, Manchester, CT

PROFIT FIRST

FOR

DENTISTS

PROFIT
FIRST
FOR
DENTISTS

PROVEN CASH FLOW
STRATEGIES FOR
FINANCIAL FREEDOM

Drew Hinrichs CPA

Barbara Stackhouse RDH, M.ED.

More to Life.Dental, Cane Ridge, Tennessee, 37013, USA

© 2021 by Union Hill Press
Barbara Stackhouse, RDH, M.Ed., and Drew Hinrichs, CPA

ISBN (paperback): 978-1-7359078-0-2
ISBN (ebook): 978-1-7359078-1-9
ISBN (audiobook): 978-1-7359078-2-6

Disclaimer:
The information contained within this book is for informational purposes only. It should not be considered financial, legal, or tax advice. You should consult with your own bookkeeper, CPA, attorney, or tax professional to make decisions for your own personal and professional needs.

Page Design & Typesetting: Chinook Design, Inc. (chinooktype.com)
Copy Editor: Zoë Bird

CONTENTS

Foreword
by Mike Michalowicz

Growing a practice doesn't often correlate with growing profit. Or even any profit, for that matter.

A few years back, I went for my regular dental checkup (I go every six months, thank you) and noticed a service technician installing a new machine next to one of the treatment rooms.

"That's my new Cone Bean X-ray machine, which has 3D CBCTs," my dentist said as he walked over to me. "It is going to allow me to make an even better assessment of people's dental situation."

"How much was it, Dr. Mark?" I said. I am more than a patient to Mark, we are longtime confidants. He knows about the work I do in the entrepreneurial space, and I likely know more about the ins and outs of his practice than his accountant.

There was a pause. Not because it was odd for me to ask that question, but because the doctor knew exactly what I was going to ask next. "It was a hundred-fifty something," he intentionally mumbled.

"One hundred fifty thousand dollars?" I reiterated.

"Well, more like $158,000, before the installation," he responded.

I won't belabor the dialog further. The machine—installed, with training for staff—came to a grand total of $162,000.

He continued, "I can't wait to start using the machine. I charge $235 for just one x-ray. This thing will pay for itself, practically overnight!"

I returned six months later, and again six months after that. The new machine sat there. I was not being patronizing, but it came across that way: "How much profit has that machine made so far?"

"I've done about three hundred scans with it so far. So, no, I'm not there yet. It's upsetting, honestly. I ran the numbers and thought it would pay for itself faster. I'm not even halfway to paying this thing off. I need more patients, Mike. I really need to grow this practice more."

After my checkup, I pulled Dr. Mark aside and asked, "Is everything okay?" It wasn't a surface-level question, but one of those where things can get real, real fast.

"I had to skip a few paychecks recently. I can't seem to grow fast enough." He paused to look around, making sure no one was within earshot. "I am looking to work part-time at another practice down the street just so I can get enough take-home for myself," he shared.

Dr. Mark's financial situation is not uncommon. A shockingly large number of dental practices are not sustainably profitable. They do everything they can to grow, to keep money coming in the door, and yet they struggle to have any form of predictable, permanent profits. But they can. And it is far easier than you can imagine.

This book has the solution Dr. Mark seeks. This book has the system that dentists need. By the time you finish reading this book, you will have a simple tool that will bring permanent profits to your practice. All you need to do is to do what this book says.

Barbara Stackhouse and Andrew Hinrichs are the leading experts in dental practice profitability. They have combined their elite accounting expertise and deep knowledge of the dental space with the Profit First system to bring what I believe is the greatest financial innovation to the dental industry. Ever.

Too many dentists are "chained to the chair," working harder and longer and trying to produce more to keep the practice healthy. With the COVID pandemic, things only got worse in terms of mounting bills and, in some cases, diminishing patient visits. The solution to the profit problem is rarely in new equipment or even more patients. The solution is in a profit system—a system in which, regardless of the number of patients you see and the variety of procedures you offer, everyone (including the owners of the practice) takes home a consistent paycheck and profit accumulates. With the Profit First for Dentists system, you will have financial predictability and accumulating cash reserves.

Without a profit system, struggling with cash flow, some dentists have tried to convince themselves that their practice isn't about money—that their work is solely about caring for their patients, even (or especially) if it is costing them to stay in business. Alas, this is a justification for improperly managing their businesses.

Serving patients at the cost of your business and your livelihood is not, I repeat, not a good practice. It is not noble. And it surely is not what your patients want. In fact, they want you to be profitable.

You can try this now. (Warning: I suggest only doing this in your mind.) Tell the next patient who comes in that you are losing money. That you can't take a paycheck. That you are scratching money together to pay for equipment and staff. Right before you start the procedure, tell them that you are worried about money and feeling desperate to get more patients (and their wallets) in the door. Again, I don't suggest you really do this. But consider this situation in your mind. Would the patient feel comfortable? Would they want to do more business with you? Or would they start to look for services elsewhere?

The fact is, your patient would freak out. Why? Because if you are financially unstable, you can't give the patient the full attention they deserve. The patient may fear you will cut corners in your need to save money. The patient knows that your mind won't be fully focused on the job at hand—it will be jumping to getting money in the door. Financial struggle results in financial worry. The solution is financial stability.

Barbara has worked in dentistry since 1988 as a hygienist, and for over sixteen years as a consultant to dentists. She has seen what it is like when a practice struggles, and when one is fiscally healthy. She knows how to make an unprofitable practice profitable. And she knows how to make a profitable practice permanently profitable.

Foreword

Drew, who specializes in serving dental practices, has been an accountant for fifteen years. He knows numbers like a dentist knows crowns. There is gold (or porcelain, for that matter) in your business, and he knows how to give you access to it.

Barbara and Drew have combined forces to revolutionize the financial health of dental practices everywhere. Right now, with this book, they will do it for you. The Profit First for Dentists system will make your practice permanently profitable. Sit back and relax; this won't hurt much at all.

Author's Note

Drew Hinrichs and I are coauthors of this book. However, as you read, you'll discover that the writing was done by me.

While the entire text is written through my voice, it includes Drew's ideas, information, and feedback throughout. The information in Chapter 9 is entirely from Drew, but largely written by me.

Barbara Stackhouse, RDH, M.Ed.

1

The Business of Owning a Dental Practice

1

DENTAL SCHOOL TO DENTAL PRACTICE

Being a million dollars in debt was not any part of Cristin's wildest dreams. All she could think about was how they'd worked so diligently on the succession plan. Every detail had been discussed and written down.

Cristin grew up in small town USA with close friends and a great education. Everyone knew everyone and looked out for each other. It was one of those idyllic places to live.

She loved learning and had good grades. Her guidance counselor pushed her to start exploring different careers, but it was a visit to the dentist that changed her direction. Dr. Bob, the only dentist she'd ever known, took an interest in her future. He invited her to come spend some time in the office to observe a day in the life. That did it! She fell in love with dentistry.

Cristin spent a lot of time in Dr. Bob's practice. He mentored her. He trained her to be a dental assistant. He encouraged her to go to dental school. He hired her when she graduated. Dr. Cristin had her name on the wall. Wow! It felt so surreal.

She and Dr. Bob discussed everything about the practice. They put a plan in place for her to eventually purchase the practice over time. It was a busy, thriving practice with longtime team members. Dr. Bob was a larger-than-life kind of guy. The team and community loved him!

They worked together well. There were so many things he was teaching her, things she hadn't learned in dental school. Those first six months out of dental school seemed to fly by. She was finally hitting her stride. The team respected her. She felt so happy, doing what she loved.

And then life changed. It changed dramatically, and in an instant. Dr. Bob suffered a massive heart attack and passed away. The shock was unbearable, the grief overwhelming. The worry set in.

She had never imagined purchasing Dr. Bob's practice this soon. She had never seen herself taking over the practice without him there to guide her. She had never planned to be a million dollars in debt. It all happened so fast, it felt like she was just going through the motions.

She couldn't shake Dr. Bob's words: "Cristin, you're the one I want to take over my practice." He trusted her. He believed in her. But it still felt like his practice. She wondered if it would ever really become her practice.

She took out a loan to purchase the practice and signed the papers. Later that week, she hosted a reception to celebrate and, with all the guests watching, she cut the ribbon for the official opening. Everyone shared in a toast. A beautiful, special evening slipped away all too quickly and there she was, alone, the last one to leave and lock the door. Before she left, she walked through the office once again, taking in the sheer enormity of it all. She came to her office, the office that once belonged to Dr.

Bob, the office where, above the door, hung the horseshoe he had given her when she was accepted to dental school. It was positioned with the opening at the top because that meant "luck" would fill it up and not drain out the bottom. She needed all the luck she could get, right then. Filled with emotion, she sat down and took in a deep breath. Thinking about the loan and all the debt was overwhelming. What in the world had she done? She felt a heavy weight, a weight she had never felt before.

When I met Dr. Cristin, her stress level was fifteen on a scale of one to ten. The debt load she carried felt crushing. She just couldn't manage to get on the other side of it. The struggle was real.

Every day she walked into the practice, her practice now, she missed him. Deep down, she was scared. Her confidence wavered. She started questioning herself. It had all happened so fast, and was certainly not like the plan they had put together.

So began Dr. Cristin's journey with dental practice debt.

DEALING WITH DEBT

Can you relate? Maybe your situation is different and you entered into a practice loan under a different set of circumstances, but debt—no matter how much—requires cash flow every month, without fail.

Having debt is pretty much a standard thing for a dental practice owner. There's dental school debt, a home loan, car loans, a practice loan, equipment loans, sometimes a practice mortgage, and often credit card debt. This is the reality many dentists live with.

With so many loans and so many payments that come around regularly every month, sometimes there's more month than money and the credit card debt rises again.

Each day, there's a constant worry just under the surface of every thought. When one thing goes wrong, there is fear of the impact. Team members feel the pressure too. The only thing most dentists know to do is just keep working.

Practice owners can begin to feel like they are chained to the chair, cranking out more and more dentistry. For sure, at least, they're always thinking about work. The stress of the debt never leaves. It's hard to relax, whether at home or away from the office. The stress is carried no matter where they go, even on vacation.

Next thing you know, a refinance of the practice loan seems to be the best option because the credit card balance just never seems to go down. Then there's the line of credit that was used to pay the tax bill. But hey, it's a better rate this time and in ten years it will all be paid off. Unless another refinance occurs.

Without a plan, debt will continue to be a challenge and can actually interfere with true growth in a practice.

BECOMING AN OWNER-DENTIST

Think back to when you first started your business. Maybe you purchased an existing practice. Perhaps you started from scratch. Remember how exciting it felt to finally have your own dental practice? Remember your dream then?

Dentistry is a good business to be in, but dentistry is also a very expensive business to be in. The cost of doing business can creep up quickly. All those dreams start to dim with the reality of the daily grind. If you're a dentist, you likely understand this. So much goes on during the typical day in a dental practice. I always say that there are a lot of moving parts, and it's hard to know what's going on at any given moment.

Your story is being written every single day in your practice. What does your story look like?

FUNDING RETIREMENT

Are you trying to save for retirement but can't seem to find the money to invest?

Financial advisors say it's best to begin saving for retirement in your early twenties, but reality has proven that, by age fifty, most people have very little or nothing saved for their fast-approaching retirement. This is a general statement across all professions. The profession of dentistry is no different. In fact, it might be worse for dentists.

Inside Dentistry published an article, "Playing the Long Game," which reported that the average age of retirement for dentists continues to increase. The article states, "Retirement is often the first time dentists will lack steady cash flow, and with no pension, they have only what they've saved and invested for this day."[1]

The key consideration is having enough cash flow long before retirement to invest some for the future. I talk to many dentists

---

[1] "Playing the Long Game," *Inside Dentistry*, Vol. 15, Issue 2 (February, 2019): https://www.aegisdentalnetwork.com/id/2019/02/playing-the-long-game

who tell me they have inadequate savings for retirement. They're banking on the sale of their practice—and they're still paying down the debt on it.

Now consider the facts reported by the American Dental Association (ADA) which indicate that "Dentists' practice ownership [is] decreasing": There are fewer younger dentists looking to purchase a practice, many dentists are working longer in their careers, and most likely those last several years of practice are at a slower pace, which leads to a decrease in the value of their practices.[2] Less value and fewer dentists looking to purchase a practice do not help those dentists trying to sell their practice to boost their nest egg for retirement!

What if it's possible to reverse the average age of retirement for dentists? Currently, in the United States, dentists' average age of retirement is sixty-nine; yet the average age of the general population at retirement is sixty-two. Seven years is a big gap.

What about you?

Where are you with your retirement savings?

Are you on track to retire when you want to?

Or will you be working until age sixty-nine, or beyond?

Are you waiting to pay off debt before you begin saving for retirement? How much time will you have left, and will you be able to adequately make up for those lost years of savings?

---

[2] "Dentists' practice ownership decreasing," *ADA News*, April 9, 2018: https://www.ada.org/en/publications/ada-news/2018-archive/april/dentists-practice-ownership-decreasing)

HAVE YOU INCREASED PRODUCTION AND COLLECTION BUT STILL FEEL STUCK?

One of the things I hear most frequently from dentists is how frustrated (and depressed) they are because they have worked hard to improve efficiency, streamline systems with their team, and produce more dentistry than ever before, yet what remains in their own pockets doesn't change much. I hear the agony in their voices. They are tired. They feel beat up. They feel betrayed.

Maybe you, like many dentists, dreamed of the autonomy and freedom of running your own business—but now here you are, owning the dream and wondering how it turned out this way. It's quite common in dentistry to just keep flying by the seat of your pants when it comes to money management.

I love the saying "you don't know what you don't know" because it helps me to understand that there's always more to learn. When you think about the business side of your dental practice, do you relate to this saying? Are you in the dark when it comes to business systems and structure?

Dental practice clinical operating systems are commonly found in most practices. Dental procedures require linear step-by-step protocols. Dentists' brains are already wired to follow systems. Wouldn't it make sense to do the same thing with the finances? Imagine having step-by-step protocols for money management. How would it feel to know how to make business decisions from accurate data?

Understanding true overhead as it relates to cash flow is the by-product of solid financial systems and strategies. As you may have experienced already, producing more does not necessarily equal increased profit. Producing more dentistry requires more supplies and more teamwork, so the overhead goes up. Logically, producing more should equal more profit. But it doesn't.

Are you tired of the hamster wheel of production? Are you tired of running from room to room? Are you tired of the production model? Until dentists completely understand how to shift to a profitability model, they will stay stuck right where they are.

GROW THE PRACTICE BY HIRING AN ASSOCIATE

On our very first call, Dr. Nate told me how he'd tried twice to grow his practice by hiring an associate. Both times it had failed miserably. And now his consultant wanted him to try one more time. He decided he didn't want to go down that road again. He started searching for something different. He knew that trying this same strategy a third time clearly wasn't going to work. He needed a different plan.

Hiring an associate or even hiring a hygienist might be exactly what you need, but how do you know before you take the plunge? As Dr. Nate found, it can be a disaster if your business is not in a position to support this additional team member plus the additional overhead beyond their compensation. If this isn't done correctly, owner compensation will take a nosedive right to the bottom of the pool. Just ask Dr. Nate and he'll confirm it!

Let's talk about logic again. Does this make sense? To grow the practice, just see more patients. To see more patients, hire more team members who are providers, like a dental associate or a hygienist. Logically this all makes sense, but what about the overhead? We've already discussed overhead and how it increases proportionately with production.

Unless you know your true cash flow numbers—how much cash comes in and how much cash goes out—you'll always be stuck thinking you can out-produce the problem. And secondly, unless you know exactly how many active patients are required per provider in your practice, you'll be guessing when it comes to the decision to hire another provider.

Not all dental practices are created equal. The number of patients per provider is inconsistent across practices. There are many variables when comparing one practice to another, especially when you are considering adding another provider. Don't just guess at this!!

If you are thinking of hiring an associate, begin by reviewing your practice numbers. How many active patients do you currently have? (Active means they have been in for care within the past eighteen months.) Also, review your schedule. How far out are you scheduled? Do new patients have to wait a long time to see you? Consider why you want to hire an associate. If you only want to do the "high level" stuff and plan to send all of the general or insurance plan dentistry to the associate, it is likely that they will get frustrated. Most associates also want to grow and learn. Will you be a mentor for them? The only way they will learn is to do some of those bigger cases, maybe with your help. Bottom line is, when you hire an associate, you will be sharing your patients with them. Do you have enough patients to give up half or more of them to an associate? How will this affect your income? Be sure you are okay with every scenario that could happen when hiring an additional provider.

BENEFIT PLANS

Even though the cost of doing dentistry continues to rise, we all know that the insurance reimbursements never seem to keep up. I continually hear from dentists who feel frustrated and totally in the dark when it comes to knowing which plans are serving them and which are hurting them.

It's almost impossible to monitor every single fee schedule in your practice—or at least it feels that way. And even if you are monitoring the fees, how do you know which insurance is feasible to accept? How do you factor in your overhead when considering the fee for a procedure?

This is where most dentists just put their heads down and work harder. They work on being as efficient as possible and secretly hope and pray they've done enough to be profitable. Since insurance companies dictate the fees, time and overhead costs are the only variables you can control.

Research says that patients with insurance are more likely to seek dental care. You certainly want patients to seek dental care, and seek it with you; however, signing up for every insurance plan may not be in your best interest. On one hand, you want the new patients, but on the other, you're stuck with the fees set forth by the insurance plan. Some plans are just not feasible to accept when you really look at profitability.

MORE NEW PATIENTS

Everyone who works in the dental field knows that, for the practice to survive, they must have a steady flow of new patients. It's a metric most practices continually measure.

More new patients equal a busier schedule. A busier schedule requires hiring more team members. Overhead goes up.

Then there's more marketing. And the cycle continues.

The bottom line is, more new patients does not necessarily equal more profit.

The dentist ends up working harder and feeling busier, yet without experiencing the reward of increased profit. This happens more than you think.

THE ROLLER COASTER OF PRODUCTION

A big challenge in dentistry is inconsistent production and collection month to month. It's quite common for practices to experience big swings in their monthly income.

A particularly slow month can trap the practice in the catch-up game for months on end. It's so frustrating.

Just paying the bills becomes the goal every month.

By the time the practice catches up, it happens again.

ECONOMIC DOWNTURNS AND OTHER CRAZY TIMES

The year 2020 was certainly one for the books! Recessions are one thing, but this pandemic took the concept of an economic shift to a whole new level. Especially for dentists.

I watched as dental practices were significantly inconvenienced and financially challenged during the shutdown. Because of some government help, the path out seemed a bit easier; but now there are predictions of another wave of shutdowns and a serious recession. Will your practice be okay? Did you ride the wave of recovery money? What happens when it's gone?

I've lived through several recessions in my lifetime. I happened to live in Phoenix during the 2008-09 real estate bust and recession, when over 250 dental practices in the Phoenix metro area closed their doors. They had no other option.

Lucky for you, the pandemic probably didn't ruin you because there were sources of assistance available.

The shutdown did not devastate you, but it certainly woke you up!

Are you realizing that you could be doing better? Are you thinking you could have been better prepared? Do you want to know for sure that your business will be fine the next time something like this happens?

Paying all the bills on time is one thing, but setting your business up to weather any recession or economic storm is completely different.

WHERE DOES ALL THE MONEY GO?

Money flows in. The team is busy collecting from insurance companies and patients. The deposits hit the bank account every week. It seems like the practice is finally getting ahead.

But at the end of the month, there's still the lingering question about where all the money went.

The accountant says things look great and the practice is doing well, but it sure doesn't feel like it.

Taxes wipe out everything that's left and then some. Now the business needs to carry some credit card debt for a few months. Unfortunately, this cycle happens every year for many practices.

It doesn't make sense. Production and collection increased this year, but where did it go?

Dr. Yvie had this very problem. She came to me as a young dentist only a year into practice ownership. She was struggling to pay herself any kind of real salary. She was tired of working hard and not knowing where the money went.

She made time for learning and dug into the Profit First for Dentists training program. We walked through the process together, so she knew exactly what to do. She opened all her bank accounts and began allocating money based on exact percentages. This allowed her to reserve money for her own salary and income tax in addition to a **Profit** Account!

Dr. Yvie was able to begin paying herself on a regular basis right away after starting her allocations. The money was there! And she had enough to pay the bills. The difference was in knowing her numbers. Finally, she didn't need to worry about having enough. She knew her allocation percentages were correct and that gave her confidence. She was also getting savvy and reducing expenses anywhere she could.

Then a crazy pandemic called COVID-19 hit our world. We all know what happened. That very week the pandemic shutdown occurred, Dr. Yvie showed up to our group support call almost in tears. Within a few short minutes, the seasoned Profit

First Dentists on the call had calmed her fears. The truth was, she did have money in the bank—money she had never set aside before. She would be fine. Yes, the Paycheck Protection Program (PPP) money would come. Yes, it would help. But, she learned, there was no reason to panic because she had already done enough with Profit First to safeguard her business in the short-term.

Fast forward to several months after Dr. Yvie returned to work, during a one-on-one coaching session. Near the end of our call, she had tears in her eyes as she said, "My business is now working for me, not me constantly working for it." She understood how the Profit First system had set her business up for success. All she needed to do was follow the system. And she is.

STORIES

These are all true stories of dentists I talk to or have worked with. You have your own story.

We all want our stories to have happy endings. As business owners, we believe in the happy ending. It's so easy to overlook parts of the real story. We end up telling ourselves it's not that bad.

The committee in your head that chatters all day long tells you lies. Maybe they are excuses.

See if you can relate.

- If I just had ____ number of new patients every month, everything would be great.

- If I ask a patient for a referral, they'll think I'm struggling and begging for patients.
- All I need to do is produce $_____ each day, week, month, or year. (You fill in the blank.)
- I think my business must be profitable because I paid income tax last year.
- Once I get the debt paid off, I'll save for retirement. I've got plenty of time.

You and I both know that the day never comes when your "if this" happens. Or maybe the day does come, but the "then this" doesn't work out.

The biggest lie of them all is believing you'll eventually figure it out on your own: All you have to do is work really hard and it will all work out.

You might just come out on the other side okay. In fact, you probably will be okay.

But do you want to be okay (mediocre), or do you want to be and do the best? If you're going to put the work in anyway, why not work smarter?

Why not factor in profit from the start? Or at least from this day forward?

A PROFITABLE BUSINESS

Unless you are a charity, owning a business means you are for-profit. In fact, setting up your business to have profit ensures that you'll be able to continue working in your dental practice business and serving patients.

Drew and I want you to understand profit.

First, let's talk about what profit is not. It is not the salary you pay yourself for being a dentist and treating patients in your office. You pay yourself for being a dentist in the practice just as you'd pay an associate dentist for working in your practice. Please understand, profit is NOT your pay.

If it's not your pay, then what is profit?

The best way to understand this is to think of yourself as working two completely different jobs for the practice. The first one is being a dentist. The second one is being a business owner and leader. You have taken the risk of business ownership. You do all the extra jobs required of you as the owner. You deserve to be paid for your time, commitment, effort, and risk. This is what profit is for.

In order to have profit pay, your business must be set up to have profit over and above the owner's pay and all the other expenses in the practice.

In the Profit First model, profit is set aside before you pay your team, yourself and all the bills. Without this additional profit, you feel like you're always chasing your tail to get ahead.

Having true profitability gives you freedom. It allows you to breathe easier when it comes to finances. Being less stressed about the money side of your business means you are more relaxed. When you are more relaxed, your patients feel it. Your team members feel it. Your family feels it. And you feel it, too.

Being profitable allows you to focus more on your patients' needs and serve them at a higher level. It also gives you added time, since you don't have to rush around so much.

Most dentists actually have it all backwards. They put their dentistry above their business needs, and I can understand why it happens. But I hope now you can begin to see why it's so important to get your business set up for profit from day one, or at least from this day forward, so you can fully focus on delivering dentistry. Get the Profit First money systems in place early on and you will have a solid financial foundation for profitability during the life of your practice.

GAAP IS WHY YOU'RE HERE

A long time ago, in the early part of the twentieth century, a set of rules was created to standardize financial reporting processes. The Financial Accounting Standards Board uses this set of rules, called the Generally Accepted Accounting Principles (GAAP), as the foundation for approved accounting methods. The core of this system has remained the same since the early 1900s.

GAAP uses the SALES – EXPENSES = PROFIT formula. Logically, this makes complete sense. All that's needed is to increase sales, spend the same or less on overhead, and keep the rest, and the owner's income should go up. But it doesn't. Oh, it looks like it on paper, but the money sure didn't show up in the bank account. The owner-dentist is left scratching their head for a minute. Because they can't figure it out, they decide to just trust the system and keep doing the same old thing.

We've been conditioned to believe that bigger is better. Go big or go home! Super-size that order! Consumerism has engulfed everything we do, including how we run our businesses.

When it looks like we have money in the account, we buy what we want and call it business expenses. This mentality kills any profit in the GAAP model. Sure, it makes us feel great for the moment, as we acquire one more shiny object, or attend one more course, or whatever the current "want" may be. (I'm sure you can fill in the blank.) The point is, we spend money because we think we have it to spend. Unfortunately, GAAP keeps the business owner in the dark most of the time, even though it works great for your accountant and bookkeeper. Remember, it was designed as the foundation for accounting methods and not as a cash flow model for you to understand how to run your business.

Profit First flips the equation and taps into our innate human behavior: SALES – PROFIT = EXPENSES. Take your profit first and then pay your expenses with what is left. It's that simple. It works because it is so simple. It works because it was designed to utilize our innate human tendencies when it comes to monitoring our money. The first thing we do when we want to know how much money we have is log into our online banking (even though the accountant tells us never to do this). When the deposits are flowing in and the dollar amount looks good, we spend. And we spend. And we spend. But when the balance gets low, it's like a panic button went off somewhere. As entrepreneurs, we kick into high gear and start doing anything and everything to generate more money. We become desperate for sales. It's the proverbial hamster wheel of business! If this is you, are you ready to get off the wheel?

PROFIT FIRST DISCLOSES THE TRUTH

As dental professionals, we know that using disclosing solution reveals all the plaque. When we want to show patients where the plaque on their teeth likes to hide, we use a disclosing agent. It's like turning on a lightbulb so the patient can see.

Some patients are eager, and want to see where their plaque hides. Others don't. Maybe it's the fear of knowing—once they know, they will have no excuses.

Profit First is like the disclosing solution for your business. Start using it and money issues are revealed It's like turning on the lightbulb so you can see what is really going on with your business finances.

Some dentists are eager and want to see, and others don't. Maybe it's the fear of knowing—once they know, they will have no excuses.

Hmmm, sound familiar?

I've been teaching and coaching dentists for a long time, more than sixteen years now. Profit First is the best system I've found to simply and quickly turn on the lightbulb so that dentists can see their businesses in a whole new way.

Are you ready to "see" what's going on in your business finances?

Is it time to change your money story?

Are you open to shifting your paradigm and paying yourself first?

Take the Dental Practice Profit Score below. This is where the rubber meets the road. Truthfully, what's your score? If you scored below 24, it's time to draw a line in the sand and get some accountability.

Send an email to Barb@BarbStackhouse.com with your score and type "Line in the Sand" in the subject line. We will respond and keep cheering you on! We'll also send you the link to download some resources to help you on your Profit First for Dentists journey.

DENTAL PRACTICE PROFIT SCORE

Using a scale of 0 to 3, rate each statement.

Not True	Seldom True	Often True	Always True
0	1	2	3

	Score
We have a detailed budget that includes income goals, profit, and expenses.	
We know the detailed cost of each service or procedure we provide.	
We monitor our overhead categories and know when we are over budget.	
We work efficiently, with as little waste as possible.	
We monitor our financial data daily, weekly, and monthly.	
We pay all our bills on time.	
We collect all receivables within thirty days.	
We monitor all purchases closely to make sure we stay within budget.	
We set aside our profit first.	
We pay the owner's income tax with ease.	
Add up your score! **Total:**	

0–10: Your business needs CPR—your finances need to be revived!
11–20: Mediocre isn't bad, but you're still in survival mode!
21–30: Cruising along, but things could still improve!

29

2

The Core Principles of Profit First for Dentists

2

THE PROFIT FIRST LIFESTYLE

Remember Dr. Cristin's purchase of Dr. Bob's practice? By the time I met her, she was feeling the heaviness of debt even more because of an economic downturn. The great recession had happened several years after she purchased the practice and the economy hadn't yet fully recovered. Her business had not only plateaued, it had taken a dip, and the bills kept coming. To her, it felt like payroll happened twice a week. The relentless cash-eating machine that was her dental practice consumed her every waking moment.

When she realized she was no longer making headway with the debt, it was worse than she expected. All that mattered now was a lifeline. Something had to change, like, yesterday. And change it did. Her landlord decided not to renew her lease. Fast forward another year and a half and she was looking at taking out a new loan, building out an office, moving, and starting over. Or at least that's what it felt like.

Just like Dr. Cristin, no matter where you find yourself in the story of your practice, there will always be bumps along the way. But there is good news. You can change your story starting right now. To change the story of your business or your life, you must first change your paradigm or belief. It's the big aha moment when you wake up and realize there must be a better way. You go searching.

Lucky for all of us, Mike Michalowicz was determined to change his story and then willing to share the process so that others could benefit too. Profit First was born out of his own desperation. It was *his* aha moment, and it happened in the middle of the night while he was watching a PBS station.

Mike was glued to the TV, learning about human behavior from a fitness expert who was explaining to the audience that quick-fix diets don't work because they're unsustainable. Boy, do fitness experts know a thing or two about that. People have been dieting for ages without success. There's so much conflicting information when it comes to losing weight. But this guy was making sense. What Mike heard was that it takes more than a quick fix when you want to make a lasting personal change. It requires simple, hardly noticeable alterations to your lifestyle. By using our ingrained habits within a new structure, we can create sustainable lifestyle fixes. So when this expert said something about small plates, Mike sat up and took notice.

We've been taught by mom to eat everything on our plate. The problem is, the size of our dinner plates has increased dramatically over the years. In the 1960s, dinner plates were eight to nine inches in diameter and were estimated to hold about eight hundred calories' worth of food. Of course that depends on your choice of food, but let's go with it. Today, in the 2000s, dinner plates are eleven to twelve inches in diameter and hold an estimated nineteen hundred calories' worth of food, nearly a whole day's quota at one meal. By switching to smaller plates, we automatically begin to eat less even though we're still following our ingrained behavior of eating everything on the plate. What a concept!

Mike was intuitive enough to translate this principle to his bank account. He realized that when his bank account was "fat" and had a lot of deposits, he would spend, spend, spend and justify the expenses as necessary. This wake-up, aha moment got him thinking seriously about his lack of money management in the past. The only system he had was the age-old GAAP formula, SALES − EXPENSES = PROFIT—the one all business owners had. But this formula wasn't working for him. The sales and expenses part worked but the profit part was missing.

Looking back, Mike realized his money had all flowed into one bank account—like the oversized plate—and he was "eating up" too much money on expenses. In essence, he was cleaning his plate or cleaning out his bank account. The idea of small plates got him thinking. If there was less cash available to pay the bills, he would automatically spend less. He wouldn't make those additional purchases the business didn't really need. It would force him to reduce overhead.

If you've been living with a roller coaster bank account in your practice, or you're left wondering where all the money goes at the end of every month, the core principles of Profit First will be music to your ears. To understand these principles, we're gonna go back to the TV show and those dieting lifestyle principles. Don't worry, it'll all make sense in the end. Buckle up and let's get started. Did you buckle up? That means it's time to put away or turn off any other distractions. If you're serious about getting your dental practice finances in better shape, you need to pay attention now.

DIETARY SCIENCE AND PROFIT FIRST

The four core principles of the Profit First system came from the exact four principles found in dietary science. Let me explain here using the dietary point of view. It's important for you to understand these principles as they relate to a healthy human being, because then it will be much easier to transfer the concept over to a healthy cash flow system.

1. **Small Plates:** Remember the size of the plate and the estimated calories consumed? It makes sense that if you use a smaller size plate, it will hold less food, you'll eat fewer calories than before, and you'll drop some pounds. Of course, it also matters what kind of food is on the plate. We'll get to that in a minute.

2. **Sequence Matters:** Think nutrition here. Eat the most nutritious food first. You know, the veggies. If you start with the nutritious veggies, you'll begin to satisfy the hunger pangs, have less room for other not-so-nutritious food, and end up eating less overall.

3. **Remove Temptation:** My husband loves ice cream. Butter pecan is his favorite. I swear he can sniff it out even when the freezer is closed. There's no hiding it. Once he knows it's there, it's not long before it's gone. But if we don't have butter pecan ice cream in the house, he's not likely to make a trip to the store to get some. He doesn't even think about it much when

there's isn't any here. The point is, when you remove the temptation by making it inconvenient, you're much less likely to go out of your way to get it.

4. **Enforce a Rhythm:** When you're hungry, you want to eat and you want it now. My daughter-in-law calls this being "hangry." Waiting until you're already hungry leads to bingeing, stuffing yourself, and eating whatever is in sight even if it isn't healthy. Instead of this cycle of hunger, it's best to eat regularly. The ideal would be to have five small meals every day so you never get hangry. This method actually leads to eating less.

Yes, I know you're not here to learn about dieting. You're reading this book because you're interested in profitability for your dental practice. Read on, because this is the good stuff. Using these same principles from the dieting world in your business puts you on the path to financial health. The good news is, it's so simple. Let's dive in and examine these four core principles of Profit First one by one.

PROFIT FIRST CORE PRINCIPLES

As in the dieting world, all of these Profit First principles are rooted in behavioral science. When you decide to work with your natural human behavior and not against it, the success rate is much greater. Makes perfect sense.

1. **Business Small Plates:** To explain this principle, we're going to explore something called Parkinson's Law: The demand for something expands to match its

supply. Remember the size of dinner plates? Smaller plates hold less food; therefore, you eat less. Large plates hold more, leading to overeating. Who hasn't gone to a family reunion potluck and filled their plate so full they are miserable after eating?

We do the same thing with time. When you're working on a project and you know you have a month to get it done, most would probably take the entire month to complete it but when you know you only have a few days, you somehow make it happen.

But the best example is toothpaste! When the tube is brand-new and full of toothpaste, most people squirt out a big long ribbon of paste to cover the brush. There's plenty available. But when the tube is nearly empty, we start twisting, rolling, and squeezing the tube, hoping to get any amount of toothpaste on the brush. When that small drop the size of half a pea lands on the bristles of the brush, we're celebrating inside like we've just won a trophy.

The lesson here is to notice how our behavior changes, based on what is available. What better lesson than 2020, the year of the pandemic that shut down dentistry as we know it for a few months. All of a sudden, there was less money coming in, so you instinctively began to cut costs. This happened before there was any word of a PPP loan or an Economic Injury Disaster Loan (EIDL), and those are really just temporary fixes anyway. When you have less, you immediately become frugal. But you also begin to get innovative and figure out new or better ways of doing things. This is a good thing—not the pandemic, but you getting frugal and innovative.

If we can all do this during a pandemic, why not make it a part of business as usual? When you have less money in your bank account, you'll get frugal and innovative. Bottom line is, you'll spend less. More on exactly how to do this in a bit.

2. **Sequence Matters:** The Primacy Effect principle helps us understand the importance of sequence and why it matters. We have a cognitive bias toward information presented first rather than later. We hold that same bias for items in the first position on a list. If you're a list maker, you'll understand. The things at the top of the list get done first.

This is good news for implementing Profit First! Sequence does matter when it comes to your money. By changing the formula to SALES − PROFIT = EXPENSES, we place profit before expenses. Seriously, it's that simple! Remember, the old way using GAAP (Generally Accepted Accounting Principles), was SALES − EXPENSES = PROFIT. This has caused entrepreneurs to place expenses before profit. The reality is, we're always waiting for the leftovers and wondering if there will be any profit left. This is not a good plan to operate on. It's actually exhausting. If you feel like you're always grinding it out at the chair, producing and collecting more only to find your income stagnating at the same level, you know what I'm talking about.

It's time to flip the equation. Make profit the primary objective.

SALES – PROFIT = EXPENSES.

Are you in?

3. **Remove Temptation:** Not keeping junk food in the house makes it less convenient to get, and we can do the same with our money. Out of sight, out of mind is the new mantra. This means we move our profit into an account to which we don't have immediate access. A lack of immediate access removes the temptation and we start making do with what we have for expenses.

   This is the fun part! Remember the formula SALES (produce and collect) MINUS PROFIT (set aside, no temptation) EQUALS EXPENSES (frugal and innovative). You follow this formula and then this amazing thing happens, and with the most perfect timing: the **Profit** Account releases some money to you, the owner. Bonus time, baby!! This is what your business is meant to do from the beginning, and now, with Profit First, it's a reality.

4. **Enforce a Rhythm:** We learned that bingeing and crashing on food is not in the best interest of our health, and the same is true for our money. Instead of

playing catch-up or going into panic mode when all the bills are due, establish a weekly rhythm and flow to the cash coming in and going out of the business. Creating consistent cash flow week in and week out removes the panic button and replaces it with peace of mind.

No longer will you need to read a cash flow or profit and loss (P&L) statement to know where you stand—and if we're being honest here, you don't do that anyway. Understanding cash flow will be as easy as opening your bank accounts and checking the balances (which is what we already do). This whole process is created using simple bank balance accounting. Profit First gives you the process and the measuring tool to make it happen.

REINVESTING IN YOUR DENTAL PRACTICE BUSINESS

It's common to think, as dental practice business owners, that we always need to be investing in the practice or the business won't grow. Let's think this through. What exactly is business growth? I'd say that business growth is an improvement of some measure of success in a business enterprise. So what exactly will you measure? Sales? Profit? Or something else?

Increasing profitability is the fastest and healthiest way to grow a business. This doesn't mean we shouldn't invest money back into the business, but it does mean we should only do so when we actually have additional profit. It's common for businesses, especially dental practice businesses, to constantly seek new technology or training as a way to grow the business. But it's also common to borrow the money to make it happen. Borrowed money is not profit to reinvest in the business.

First things first, generate profit. Good old cash flow profit will increase the value of the practice more than anything else. Consistent profit gives us the power and freedom to reinvest at a healthy rate. Profit First is the mechanism for healthy, consistent growth because it forces us to examine the business's expenses. When you implement Profit First, you'll find yourself being innovative and frugal as you learn what is really going on with your finances.

The bottom line is, it is possible to do both: generate a profit and reinvest at the same time. In fact, it's a business-healthy option. Remember, though, profit comes first. I'm talking about true profitability here, not some number on a profit and loss report that doesn't make sense to you because you don't have that amount of money sitting in your account. I hope by now this has piqued your interest and that you'll read on, because the good how-to stuff is what the rest of this book is about. Drew and I are here to help you fully implement Profit First in your dental practice. We believe it is the simplest and fastest way to eradicate dental entrepreneur poverty.

GETTING YOUR ACCOUNTANT ON BOARD

Now is the time to talk to your accountant and get them on board with Profit First. Profit First will change nothing about how they conduct their accounting practices, but it will change everything about how you learn to have cash flow. We've included some questions here to help you in the conversation with them.

5 Critical Questions for a Profit Ready Dental Practice Accountant

1. Of your existing clients, how many post consistent quarterly profit?
2. Do you have a bank-based management tool?
3. How many Profit First rollouts have you completed for dentists?
4. Do you understand the unique challenges facing dental practice owners and utilize a proper Chart of Accounts for Dentists?
5. How many of the clients you serve are dentists?

If your accountant is supportive of the Profit First system, they will immediately understand the benefit to you, the business owner. Again, we want you to understand that the Profit First system changes nothing in terms of how they practice accounting for your business. It has everything to do with how you monitor your cash flow and make informed decisions about your finances.

We (Drew, CPA, and Barb, Profit First coach) are both certified Profit First professionals. We both understand our role as supportive of the other. In fact, this kind of collaboration is the best option a dentist could hope for and we can prove it with our mutual clients.

Over time, Dr. Cristin had worked with several different accountants. It turns out that none of them were on board with or supportive of the Profit First system. When Drew and I began collaborating together as Profit First Professionals, Dr. Cristin finally found what she was looking for: a team of professionals to support her efforts. Having a supportive team is critical. Each person on the team has their role and understands how that role supports the entire process. It's not a competition. It's a supportive, collaborative environment built on trust. As your business grows and you increase profitability, there will be other trusted professionals on this team as well.

3

Using Bank Accounts to Your Advantage

UNDERSTANDING THE REASON FOR
MULTIPLE BANK ACCOUNTS

Imagine it's Thanksgiving Day. The turkey is on a big tray in the middle of the table. Your friends and family are seated around the table and they're starving. So they each pick up their fork and knife and dive right into that turkey, cutting it up, hacking off pieces and shoving them in their mouths. No, no, no, that's not how we do it! No. We don't eat from the big tray. Instead, we carve the turkey into smaller portions and place them on smaller plates, one for each person seated at the table.

Imagine your bank account is like the turkey on the big tray. With Profit First, all the money flows into one account called the **Income** Account, but we don't pay the bills from this account. That would be like eating from the big tray. Instead, we allocate by percentage to additional bank accounts, each set up for a specific purpose—small plates. These are the **Profit**, **Owner's Compensation**, **Tax**, and **Operating Expenses** Accounts. Once money is allocated and transferred to its "small plate" account, it is only used for that purpose.

Something amazing happens when we divide up the money from the **Income** Account and move it to additional "small plates" accounts. That something amazing is a change in behavior. Yes, I know it's difficult to wrap your head around how much of an impact this has on the ways you think and behave with your money. But believe me, it does. It's like some sort of magic happens when you totally commit to the process and make the allocations.

Dr. Amy began working with me and followed my training by opening the additional accounts, but when it came time to make all the allocations, she only made the Profit allocation. For whatever reason, she just didn't think the other allocations would make that big of a difference. She liked having the **Profit** Account and began funding it every week. That alone made a significant difference, but she wasn't experiencing the full benefit of utilizing all of the accounts.

Finally, some time later, after making a quarterly tax deposit, Dr. Amy decided to add the **Tax** Account to her allocations. Once she started this additional allocation, something remarkable happened. She suddenly realized the power of this additional bank account. Her tax liability was now funded and she never had to worry about it again. She told me later that she never realized what a big impact this would have on her.

Money is emotional. Everyone has feelings about money. It doesn't matter if there's a lack of or an abundance of money; either state produces feelings. One of the reasons Profit First works is the positive emotional response that occurs when we see the cash in all our accounts. It's hard to describe what happens, and Dr. Amy was no exception. In her words: "I know you told me to open these accounts and start allocating money, but

I didn't think it was a big deal. Now that I'm making the allocations, I get it. Now I really understand."

Here's why it's so hard to describe. The human brain is wired in one area for emotional responses and a totally different area for language. The inner or limbic brain is where emotional responses originate, but there are no language skills in this area. We cannot formulate words from the limbic brain.

We also know that behaviors are largely controlled by emotional responses or connections. Profit First is a behavioral system It works with our natural human behaviors. It is natural to log into your bank account and check the balance when you want to make a purchase. But when you have only one account this is a problem, because you have no way of understanding your true cash position. With the Profit First system of multiple accounts, each created for a specific purpose, it's simple to review the balance in each account and get a quick, accurate picture of the cash position. When cash reserves begin to build, a positive emotional response occurs. It's like a reward for the behavior of making allocations.

Let's get practical here and talk about why having multiple bank accounts makes such a big difference. Remember Parkinson's Law? The demand for something expands to match its supply. Translate this to your bank account. The more money available in the account, the more we spend. Naturally, when the money is divided into four additional accounts, there's less money in each account. Less money means we spend less. It forces us to be more resourceful—and we know, after a pandemic-forced shutdown in 2020, that we can do it! Each of these accounts is also tagged for its specific purpose: Profit, **Owner's Compensation, Tax,** or **Operating Expenses.** Once the money is allocated to an account, it can only be used for that purpose. Knowing that all of these areas are covered actually brings greater peace of mind to money management.

All right, I know you want the details. Let's go over all the bank accounts you'll need to set up.

THE FIVE CORE ACCOUNTS
Income Account

The sole purpose of this account is to receive all deposits from any sales or services provided. This includes patient payments via cash, check, or credit card, plus all insurance payments received. The money accumulates in the account until it's time to allocate by percentage and make transfers to the other accounts. Once allocations are made, the process starts over, with all deposits just hanging out here for the week until it's time to allocate money again. We do not pay any bills from this account—remember, that would be like eating turkey from the big tray, and not even the Griswolds would do that!

> **Important Tip:** Combining the **Income** and **Operating Expenses** Accounts does not give you the clarity you need to fully understand bank balance accounting, and here's why. Each bank account has a specific purpose and gives clarity about the money held for that purpose. When you mix two or more accounts together, you also mix up their purposes

and things get fuzzy. So which do you want? Confusion or clarity? You choose! If you want clarity, open the accounts and use each for its intended purpose.

One other option: I learned this from Dr. Rebecca, so I take no credit. When she decided she wanted some help using Profit First in her practice and chose me to help her, we discussed this very thing: what accounts she would need. When we discussed the **Income** Account and how all the money would flow into it, she explained how her current system works. She has a bank account set up for each dental insurance benefit company, and all money received from a certain company flows to that account only. Once a week, the money in all of these insurance deposit accounts automatically shifts into to the big **Income** Account. Then she makes her allocations and transfers money to her other four core accounts. The advantage of this method is the ability to balance daily with all the deposits. And you can do the same with all of your credit card deposits. I love it when systems make things so simple to monitor. This is a great system of checks and balances.

Profit Account

I find that most dentists I talk to are confused about exactly what profit is. Let's clear up that confusion. Profit is the money set aside to provide a cash distribution to the owner(s) of the practice at the end of every quarter. It's the reward for taking the risk and working all those additional hours to run your company. You invest a lot of time and money into this business, and the **Profit** Account provides you with a return on that investment. Besides loving dentistry and what you do, why else would you invest so much of yourself?

> **Important Tip:** Placing importance on profit actually makes you a better dentist. Let me explain. When you know the finances are in order, the business is profitable, the bills are paid, and you are rewarded for your efforts, your stress level goes down significantly. Less stress about money puts you in a position to relax more, connect with your patients, and focus on the dentistry you provide. When you put your profit first, you also put your patients first. Think about it: Your patients *want* you to be profitable, because they want a relaxed and happy dentist doing their dentistry!

Owner's Compensation Account

The purpose of this account is to pay the owner-dentist who works in the practice seeing patients and doing dentistry. Think of it this way: If you worked as an associate dentist somewhere else, you'd get paid for the services you delivered. The same is true in your own practice. You get paid for the dentistry you do. The **Owner's Compensation** Account is there to hold the money that will be used for this purpose.

> **Important Tip:** This account is used only for owner's compensation and is not used to pay an associate doctor who may be part of your team. The associate is considered an employee. If they were to eventually purchase a part of the practice, they would then become an owner or part owner and be paid from the **Owner's Compensation** Account. Of course, this may change the percentage for the allocation. You never want to mix owner and team compensation in one account. Remember, you lose clarity when you do this.

Tax Account

The main purpose of the **Tax** Account is to fund the owner's income tax. It is also used to hold the money for any other state or local business taxes. Whether you pay yourself via regular payroll or draw from the business for your personal expenses, you will pay income tax on that money. In fact, the money your business generates will be considered your income and you will be taxed on it. This gets real sticky because you don't always "see" the income generated. Here's a great example: Your business must generate enough income to pay the debt payment on your practice loan. The principal portion of your practice loan payment is considered your income—not an expense—and you are paying taxes on the money that you just paid to the bank. No one ever explains this when you take out the loan. If tax time is a surprise every year, this might be why.

> **Important Tip:** The Tax Account is for the owner's income tax and is not used for team payroll taxes or sales tax (if you sell products). Team payroll taxes and sales tax are part of your general practice operating expenses.

Before we go any farther, I want to step back for just a moment and revisit the Profit First formula:

$$\text{SALES} - \text{PROFIT} = \text{EXPENSES}$$

We've covered two parts of this equation so far. Your **Income** Account holds all the money from sales in your practice. The **Profit** Account, **Owner's Compensation** Account, and **Tax** Account all benefit the owner and are funded from the overall profitability of the company. This covers the profit part of the equation. All we have left is the expenses. See how simple it is?

Operating Expenses Account

The purpose of this account is to set aside money to pay all the bills, loan payments, team payroll, supplies, and lab expenses. All business operating expenses are paid from this account. Remember, you will have already set aside money in your **Profit, Owner's Compensation**, and Tax Accounts, so the remaining amount in this account is available to pay the bills or make purchases you need for your business. The key point is this: When you want to make a purchase, you can open this account, see how much money you have, assess the situation based on what bills are due, and quickly determine if your business can support the purchase or not. This is the instant clarity that will save you from overspending. Your bank account will tell you whether or not you can afford something. Once you implement Profit First and learn how easy the system is, there's no turning back. You're in the driver's seat now!

> **Important Tip:** Remember to include all debt payments (principal plus interest) in the operating expenses. These payments will not show up on your profit and loss report as an expense, but in the Profit First for Dentists world, they are big expenses that must be accounted for. They are always included here in the operating expense category.

LESS IS MORE

The phrase "less is more" was adopted by architect Ludwig Mies van der Rohe in 1947 to explain his minimalist style. It is used to express the view that a minimalist approach to artistic or aesthetic matters is more effective. Over the years, we have adapted the phrase for use in many aspects of life, including finances. The minimalist approach supports the Profit First idea well. I'm not asking you to clean house and only keep a minimal amount of things. However, I do think having a "less is more" mindset can assist you in determining whether a possible purchase is a want or a need in the moment. This is especially important when you are working hard to reduce expenses.

Here are some reasons why "less is more":

- Having less stuff creates more space. (This is so true for countertop space.)
- Spending less means you have more money. (Think **Profit** Account.)
- Less furniture means more room. (Your reception area will look bigger with less in it.)
- Less time on social media means more time with family or reading a great book.
- Less stress means you'll probably sleep better.
- Less time talking means more time listening.

Create your own "less is more" list and start paying attention to it.

There's a great book called *Essentialism: The Disciplined Pursuit of Less* by Greg McKeown. In it, he says, "Essentialism isn't about getting more done in less time. It's about getting only the right things done." He goes on to explain that this is a systematic discipline for determining what is absolutely essential, then going about eliminating the rest so you can truly focus on what really matters. What if you did this with your expenses? What would you keep? What would you let go of? What really matters in your dental practice?

From an energy perspective, this idea of "less is more" makes even greater sense. We know that everything in the universe has a certain level of energy. Money is energy. It is used in the exchange for something else that also holds a level of energy. The way we manage money either disperses energy outward or converts it for use within. When your finances are in chaos and you don't know where you stand, money seems to fly out faster than it comes in; there is a dispersion of energy. Now imagine: If you have a simple system in place for your money and it begins to grow, you've harnessed that energy and converted it into something greater. Systems and order will always harness the power of energy and use it to a greater capacity. It's common for dentists to create systems and protocols for all the different procedures in their practice. Everything is very linear and you're used to step-by-step directions.

Dentistry is very structured.

What about you and your practice?

What about your money?

Do you have any money systems in place?

Do you have simple money systems that are working well?

Using multiple bank accounts in the Profit First for Dentists system sets you up for your money to convert a greater amount of energy. It's a simple way to begin utilizing the strengths found in the "less is more" and "essentialism" concepts. It moves your finances from chaos to order, step by step by step. Now is the time to take the first step! Are you ready?

BABY STEPS

As with anything new, it's best to start small and expand from there. This is not a go big or go home system; in fact, that would probably be too big of a shock and you'd abandon the system altogether. We've put together some easy first steps for you to follow.

1. Commit to the process! New things always come with resistance. When the going gets tough, many give up. We ask you to stay with it and trust that it will work because we know it does.

2. Next, GET YOUR BUTT to the BANK and open a business SAVINGS account. Name it PROFIT. Simple enough. That's all you need to get started. *Stop everything and do it now.* Call your banker and set up an appointment or, better yet, see if you can start the process online.

3. Every week, starting as soon as your **Profit** Account is set up, transfer just 1% of all collections that week to this savings account. Only transfer money into this account; NEVER move money out of it. Leave it alone for now. I'll teach you the next steps a bit later in the book, but for now, let it sit there.

BONUS:

Email a selfie of you with this book in front of your bank when you go to open your accounts so we can share it on our social media to celebrate your achievement with you.

Email the selfie to Barb@BarbStackhouse.com and we'll send you a sample chart of accounts to help you get organized.

4

Sequence and
Timing Matter

4

SEQUENCE AND THE PRIMACY EFFECT

I know without a doubt that, as a dentist, you understand the importance of sequence. Pretty much everything done in dentistry is a step-by-step process. If you messed up the sequence of steps in a procedure, the outcome would not be what you expected or it would be a complete failure. Have you ever forgotten to take the impression for the temp before you started the prep? Out-of-sequence mistakes can ruin your day. The same is true when following a recipe. If you decide to change the order of the steps in a recipe, the outcome would either be inconsistent or likely be considered a failure. It's easy to grasp this concept when it comes to physical processes and procedures, but what about when applied to behavior?

If you are a person who makes to-do lists, you'll probably understand how this affects behavior. It's typical for the things at the top of the list to get done first. They take priority. Chances are, whatever is at the top of the list was placed there because it's the thing you really want to get done. It's important enough to be placed first. This is called the "primacy effect." It's a cognitive bias toward initial stimuli or observations. In other words, the things that come first are more likely to be remembered or acted upon. By putting something first on a list, it automatically gives you the cognitive bias to remember it and ultimately do it.

By consciously putting something in the first position, we place more importance on it and, in effect, create a different behavior. We can use the primacy effect to change behavior. Let's go back to the Profit First formula. Remember, the "old" way, created in the early 1900s, is SALES - EXPENSES = PROFIT. In this formula, expenses are placed before profit, so our behavior will follow the same lead. We'll keep working and working to pay the bills. Ever feel that way? It leads to wondering where the profit goes. By flipping the equation to SALES - PROFIT = EXPENSES, a little bit of woo-woo psychology and the primacy effect take over. We've now placed profit before expenses. Psychologically, we've said it's important. Our behavior will follow the shift in belief. Reality and challenges will still show up, but now we'll stop and reflect on our behavior because we have a system with a sequence that matters.

I remember when Dr. Cristin was just getting started with Profit First. She emailed me in a panic because it was midweek (not time to make allocations or do transfers), yet she needed to pay bills and there wasn't enough in the Operating Expense Account to cover them. There was money in the **Income** Account, though, and she wanted to use it. This was her first moment of truth with Profit First. And this is when she learned that sequence matters.

My reply to her was this: "As long as you use your allocation percentages and follow the sequence to make the transfers into all four additional bank accounts, you may proceed." One of the first things to understand with Profit First is that the order in which you transfer money from the **Income** Account to the other four accounts is super-duper important. If you get stuck (we all do at some point) and decide to just use all the money in the **Income** Account and transfer it to the **Operating Expenses** Account so you can pay your bills, you've defeated the purpose. Please don't ever do this.

If you must pay bills and you need money in the **Operating Expenses** Account to do so, then use the money in the **Income** Account, but always allocate to all four accounts in this order: **Profit, Owner's Compensation, Tax,** and **Operating Expenses.** You also want to use the correct percentage for each account. Don't skimp on any other accounts just to put more in your **Operating Expenses** Account. We're gonna talk about how to determine the correct percentages in another chapter, but for now, just know it's important to commit to following the percentages.

I want you to understand why this principle is so important. Profit First means just that: Take your profit first. Remember, profit in the new equation includes profit, owner's compensation, and taxes. It's all about your business working for you! If you don't take care of you and your finances, no one else will. There is no one who will care more for your money than you.

There's a big fat lie about always putting the patient first. Yes, I said it. It's time to take a good hard look at you. If you are experiencing money issues, they will trickle down to every aspect of your life and practice. If you don't stop right now and decide that this is important—more important than your patients, right at this moment—you will continue to stay stuck, always trying to dig out of the financial pit. When you finally decide—and take action—to be profitable from this day forward, peace of mind will be your friend. When you have peace of mind and less stress (because you took care of your money first), you'll be much more present and purposeful with your patients. Get this monkey off your back so you can serve your patients at a higher level. The bottom line is this: If you want to have better relationships with your team and your patients, you must take care of you. This includes all aspects of your life, including your finances.

FROM THE "OLD" FORMULA TO THE "NEW"

It's common for dentist-entrepreneurs to work, work, work, serve their patients, take care of their teams, and then one day wake up and realize the finances are a mess. If you can relate, please do not beat yourself up. Dentistry is a demanding profession. The clock is ticking all day long while you race against it—or at least that's what it feels like. This is what happens when you're stuck in the GAAP formula.

Time for some history. The US government believed that part of the reason for the stock market crash in 1929 was the less-than-above-board practices of some publicly traded companies. In order to regulate these practices, a uniform system was created. That system includes GAAP, the general formula of which is, again, SALES – EXPENSES = PROFIT. Since that time, businesses large and small have been using this formula because it's all we've known. Accountants had to adopt this process to be legal with the government when filing returns. However, you as a business owner have the freedom to choose the formula you will use for managing your money. Just to be clear, your internal money management system will not affect the system your accountant uses. The accountant will still use the GAAP method to keep your business legal with the government, and you can use the Profit First method to keep you in the know and keep your business cash flow healthy.

The formula and system you choose to run your business and understand its finances are based on what makes sense to you. You must have the ability to quickly assess your financial position and make decisions. Traditional accounting requires analyzing multiple reports to extrapolate information and make some sense of it. If you're comfortable with that and it's working for you, by all means, continue on. This book and the Profit First system are for those of us who need and want a simpler system, with immediate feedback for our decision-making process.

Since you do have a choice, why not use a proven system of profitability?

As Dr. Cristin says, "Since starting Profit First, my income is increasing. I have never viewed money as fun, and Profit First is changing the way I view money. I get excited each week to make my transfers. I know exactly what is there to pay myself, taxes, and my bills. It makes finances so easy. They should teach this in dental schools. We would have way more dentists enjoying dentistry and being profitable."

WHY A RHYTHM IS IMPORTANT

Mike Michalowicz, in the original *Profit First* book, relates this idea of establishing a rhythm to the dieting world. Remember the small plates from Chapter 2? The diet industry has figured out that when you eat smaller amounts (small plates) more often (rhythm), your hunger levels stay in check, your metabolism increases, you are much less likely to overeat, and desired weight loss is easier to achieve.

As a dentist, you also need a healthy rhythm for cash management. The frequency of this rhythm affects the success of Profit First for Dentists. I have found that a once-a-week rhythm seems to work best for a dental practice. Every week, allocate by percentage from the **Income** Account to your four other core accounts. Easy to say, but how do you do it? How do you discipline yourself to do the allocations? What is the motivator?

Since motivation comes from within, you must know what motivates you. Just because we tell you to do this weekly doesn't mean you will do it. The first step is to sit down and write a list of reasons why you are reading this book and why you are interested in the Profit First system. Don't shy away from this. Don't judge yourself for your true reasons. Remember, it's okay to take care of you first because then you'll be in much better shape to take care of others.

As a dental healthcare provider, it's easy to get sidetracked into believing it's your duty to take care of everyone else first. When you are scheduled to see patients, it is time to put them first. When you are working on your business—not in it—it is time to put you first. Are you scheduling time to work on your business just as you schedule time to work in it, seeing patients? My guess is that most dentists do not block out time in their schedules to do the business work. If you're not blocking out time for this, my guess is that you're running your business by the seat of your pants.

Where you are today is the sum total of the decisions you have made up to this point. Where you are six months, a year, or five years from now will be shaped by the decisions you make today. Decide carefully. If you don't have a cash flow money management system, get one. Just like every other system in your practice, it's there for a reason. Chances are, you are reading this book because the idea of a cash flow system in which you actually take your profit first might be appealing to you. Deep down, you know that if you could get a handle on the money, your life would be better in so many ways. Take some time to identify what this looks like for you. How would your life be better with a cash flow system like Profit First?

Remember, there must be motivation to do this, and a reward to be experienced, or chances are it won't last. It's easy to make a commitment to do the weekly allocations, but it's going to take more than a commitment to do it for the long haul. There's proof all around for this—just look at the dieting world or the fitness world! I can attest to the challenge of steady commitment when it comes to both. I have good intentions to go to the gym on a regular basis. This usually happens about the first of January every year. Can you relate? I have good intentions to eat healthy, but then something happens and I get off track. Again, can you relate?

Knowing your why—getting in touch with your inner motivation at a deep level—is key to making any kind of significant change last. Change requires the rhythm of habit. When the habit or action is first on your list of importance and is done rhythmically, the reward or the desired outcome will appear effortless.

HOW THE WEEKLY RHYTHM WORKS

Implementing Profit First in a dental practice is best achieved using a weekly rhythm. This means allocating money once a week from the **Income** Account to the other four core accounts: **Profit, Owner's Compensation, Tax,** and **Operating Expenses.** After the allocations are completed, simply go about paying the bills as usual from the **Operating Expenses** Account.

All the deposits flow into the **Income** Account. At the end of the week, determine the total of the deposits for that week. Remember, this amount may be different than what the practice software says was collected because some deposits may still be pending or have yet to show up in the online banking register. To make allocations, the cash must be there in the **Income** Account and available to use.

Use the total of deposits to calculate the exact percentage to allocate to each account. (We will go over how to determine these percentages later in this book.) Then determine the dollar amount. Once the dollar amount is determined for each account, simply transfer the money from the **Income** Account to each of the accounts respectively, in this order: **Profit, Owner's**

Compensation, Tax, and **Operating Expenses.** Honestly, it's that simple and literally takes minutes each week.

The key to all this is to take action every week. Don't skip a week because the deposits amount to less that week and you think you'll just wait to build up your **Income** Account more. Remember, you are creating a habit, and this habit is weekly. Also remember, there is a reward for you. Every week you'll be reminded of your why, your motivator, your reward as you make your allocations and transfer the money.

If you've been haphazard in managing your money and paying the bills up till now, this rhythm will get you on the right track fast. Another benefit to this weekly rhythm is, you will actually spend less time managing your money. Yes, that's correct. Who has time to waste on financial management tasks? Once you get the hang of it, figuring out the dollar amount of the allocations and making the transfers will take less than fifteen minutes of your time. If you pay your own bills, you'll pay some each week and will never again have to deal with a mountain of bills that you put off paying because it's a time-suck. Better yet, someone else is helping you pay the bills and this makes their life easier, too.

When or if you start to question whether or not you'll do the allocations and transfers, remember this: Profit is not an event. You're not going to wake up some day and miraculously have profit. Profit is part of every single deposit made to the **Income** Account. Profit is a habit. Profit is a mindset. Profit happens every day, every week, every year when you use the Profit First for Dentists system.

TAKE ACTION

If you haven't done so already, now is the time to set up the remaining core bank accounts. If you've been following along and taking action, by now you already have a **Profit** Account. It's time to expand and open the other accounts. Here's a list of the accounts and my suggestions for what type of account to open for each.

1. **Income Account:** business checking account
   (This could be your current business account, especially if automatic deposits are set up for this account.)
2. **Profit Account:** savings account
3. **Owner's Compensation Account:** business checking account or savings account
   (Keep in mind, a savings account may have no more than six withdrawals per month.)
4. **Tax Account:** savings account
5. **Operating Expenses Account:** business checking account
   (This could be your current business account if there are a lot of automatic payments from this account and it would be easier to change the automatic deposits to another account.)

Take some time to determine your own personal motivation for implementing the Profit First system in your business. Write it down. Put it in a place where you will see it often. Remember it and go over it daily.

- Decide what day of the week you will do your allocations and make the transfers via online banking.
- Make the transfers in the correct order.
- Decide what day of the week you will pay the bills. Block out this time in your calendar.
- Make profit a priority and take care of you first so you are fully present for everyone else!
- Figure 4.1 is a diagrammed model to explain the process.

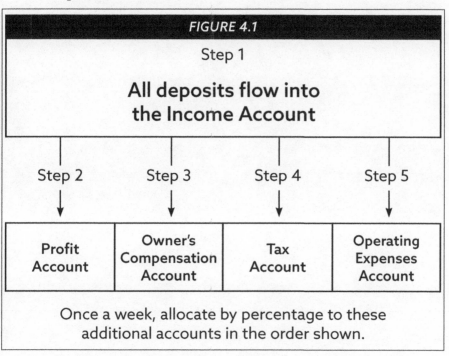

FIGURE 4.1

Step 1

All deposits flow into the Income Account

Step 2	Step 3	Step 4	Step 5
Profit Account	Owner's Compensation Account	Tax Account	Operating Expenses Account

Once a week, allocate by percentage to these additional accounts in the order shown.

Keep reading: Chapter 6 is where I explain how to do the Self-assessment. This assessment details how to figure out the percentage for each category of the allocations. At this point, it's most important to understand the purpose of the additional accounts and the order in which to do the allocations. As long as you are tracking with the purpose for each account and the specific order in which to make allocations and transfers, you're good. Read on!

5

Remove Temptation

5

A BIG TEMPTATION IN DENTISTRY

Have I got a deal for you! Except there's no game show involved.

Continuing education (CE) can be one of the most tempting ways to spend, for a dentist. Here's how it typically goes. A dentist attends a course and is convinced this new offering will transform their practice. The excitement of it all has them dreaming of helping patients in a new way. But they'll need all the equipment to get started. And if they make the purchase while they're at the meeting, they will save so much money. Logically, it makes sense. The practice income will increase once this protocol is fully implemented. The equipment purchased is supposed to pay for itself.

Has this ever happened to you? Continue on and see if this also sounds like something you've experienced after a CE course with "shiny objects."

You're so excited on Monday morning following the amazing CE course and can't wait to tell your team all about what you've just learned. But they don't seem to pick up on your excitement. Secretly they are hoping that in a few weeks, things will get back to normal and this new idea will be lost in the shuffle of busy practice life. The learning and the new processes just never seem to be fully implemented. There may be some effort, but not enough to sustain them long-term. Perhaps the team doesn't fully understand. Perhaps they are not motivated. For whatever reason, the equipment and training now sit on the shelf, so to speak.

This scenario happens all too often. I'll admit there are many dentists who do involve their team, who do get the training and equipment off the shelf and working well. However, I know that the reality is far too often the scenario I described above.

The CE (continuing education) course has now become the CE (cash evaporator) of your business. Poof! There it went. It's like the money just flew out the door and you have nothing to show for it. Where's the return on investment (ROI) you were promised? Why isn't this equipment paying for itself like you thought it would? You are left wondering what just happened. And the worst part is, you brush it aside and get back to doing dentistry—staying busy, busy, busy.

There's nothing wrong with taking a high-level CE course and making a purchase of required equipment to up-level your service offering. The problem is when there's no plan in place ahead of time. Making a knee-jerk or last-minute decision to make a big purchase at a course or a meeting because it's the best deal is probably not the best way to approach adding a new service. The temptation at these courses and meetings is high.

Temptation leads to justification. If you find yourself justifying a purchase, you are being sucked in by temptation. If this is you, and you know who you are, take notice now because this will impact how you implement Profit First in your business.

KICK TEMPTATION TO THE CURB!

If you are tempted at the CE course, you may also be tempted by money sitting in several bank accounts. Using the Profit First system correctly means money will accumulate in the **Profit** Account and the **Tax** Account. This is a good thing, right? So how can that be tempting? Here's how. When there's not enough money in the **Operating Expenses** Account to pay all the bills, it's natural to start looking around for any available cash. Sitting right there under our noses in the **Profit** and **Tax** Accounts is cold, hard cash. It's all too easy to justify using it to pay the bills. We end up telling ourselves we'll pay it back next week or next month and boom, there we go transferring the money to the **Operating Expenses** Account so we can pay the bills. Can I say, epic fail at Profit First? I urge you, please don't do this!

This is the moment when the business is screaming! It's telling you there's a problem. The problem will not go away if you ignore it. Just like decay on a tooth, it will likely get worse if it's not addressed. Now is the time to understand the Profit First system and how it's designed to help practice owners get to the truth about their relationship with money.

Everyone has their own unique relationship with money, including you. It forms over your lifetime. You probably adopted money beliefs from your parents or grandparents. You may have looked to a mentor for financial guidance. The way you handle money and the way you understand how money flows in your business and life may be a big mystery to you. It's interesting how we adopt beliefs and take action almost subconsciously when it comes to money. And, back to my earlier point, we justify all the actions. This makes it even harder to face the truth. A strong temptation is to keep the emotions and beliefs buried. For the moment that seems the easiest thing to do, but where will you be six months or a year from now?

We assume you're reading this book because you are interested in Profit First and are somehow connected to dentistry. You want to know how this works in a dental practice business. Drew and I will also assume that you want to succeed at implementing the system. You do not want to fail. Perhaps you've even tried doing this before and fell short. We're writing this book because we want you to be successful with Profit First. We've seen how it transforms our clients' practices and lives. And we know without a doubt that it can help you too!

Kick temptation to the curb! Because Profit First is a behavioral system, it actually helps you move beyond the temptation and instills new belief patterns around finances. It does require a commitment from you to follow the system as it was designed. If you've drawn your line in the sand already and have fully committed to uncovering your own financial truth, stay focused and temptation will no longer be your enemy.

The Profit First system is designed to squash the temptation to borrow from the **Profit** or **Tax** Accounts, but if you know you would be tempted to use the money in these accounts when or if the **Operating Expenses** run low, listen up: You will need to open two extra accounts at a second bank across town where it will be harder to access the money. These are called the No-temptation Accounts! In addition to the five accounts at the main bank, you'll have two more accounts (in a bank across town) to hold the money in the **Profit** and **Tax** Accounts. Remember, the **Profit** and **Tax** Accounts will accumulate money over time and are the most tempting to borrow from when or if your **Operating Expenses** Account gets low. Once a week, after you make all the allocations and transfers using the accounts at your main bank, you will then move the money from the main bank **Profit** and **Tax** Accounts to the respective accounts at the bank across town. Think of these accounts as "holding" accounts. If you choose to utilize the No-temptation Accounts, you'll have a total of seven bank accounts instead of five.

These two extra No-temptation Accounts in a bank across town are there to protect you from yourself. They are designed to make it difficult for you to access the money so that, if a day comes when you run short of money in the **Operating Expenses** Account, you will have to think twice about stealing from yourself. Yes, I did say stealing from yourself. Would you steal from a friend if you had access to their bank account? Heavens, NO! Then why in the world would you even consider stealing from yourself?

It amazes me how awfully we treat ourselves. Maybe it's time for some self-love. You may not have managed money well in the past. You may be guilty of robbing Peter to pay Paul. You may have even stolen from yourself in the past. That is all the past. Today is a new day. Today you have an opportunity to forgive yourself for not knowing how to do this differently. But now you know there's a better way. No more excuses! You are smart and you are worthy, and you can create the most amazing, profitable dental practice with a true passion for and focus on serving your patients.

DO YOU NEED THE TWO NO-TEMPTATION ACCOUNTS?

Drew and I work with many clients who have never set up the two No-temptation Accounts and they're doing just fine. We do recommend these accounts, but they are not required in order for you to be successful with the Profit First system. Only you can determine if these accounts are required for you. Our clients who have chosen not to set up these two additional accounts at another bank each have their own reason.

When considering these two accounts for yourself, think about the following:

- How tempted are you to "steal" from your personal savings when your checking account balance is low?
- Is it common for you to use a credit card and then not have the funds to pay it off at the end of the month, thus leading you to "borrow" or "steal" from your savings?
- What are your thoughts about making a purchase when you see a large sum of money in your bank account?
- Are you surviving month to month or week to week?

If you are worried you might "steal" from yourself, by all means, open the additional accounts at another bank. Set up these accounts so that you must actually go to the branch to withdraw money from them. Make it as difficult as possible to get to the money. Take every action possible to reduce the temptation to use this money for any other purpose than that for which it was intended.

If you know without a doubt that you will never "steal" from these accounts, you may choose to keep the profit and tax money in the respective accounts at your main bank. You may have many reasons for wanting to keep all your accounts at one bank, and that is understandable. It is nice to see all the accounts in one place. It seems much easier to manage all the accounts if they are at only one bank. Maybe it feels like a big inconvenience to use a second bank, especially if you are confident you'll never touch that money for any other purpose.

YOU DECIDE FOR YOU

Before you get started with Profit First, and prior to facing any challenges, it's a good idea to decide ahead of time if you need these two additional No-temptation Accounts at a different bank. On the next page is a little quiz to help you determine what's best for you.

NO-TEMPTATION SCORE

On a scale of 1 (least tempting) to 10 (most tempting), rate yourself on the following statements. Be totally honest with yourself. Better yet, ask someone who knows you well to rate you at the same time.

Very low temptation. I'd never use this money for a different purpose.	I'd consider it but would be unlikely to follow through.	I'd give it serious thought and would probably use the money after considering all my options.	High-temptation. Yes, I'd use the money because I need it right now.
1–2	3–5	6–7	8–10

Score

If I see money sitting in any account and I need it to pay bills, I will likely use it.	
If I have an "off" month and my production and collection are significantly down, I will be okay with using money from my Profit or Tax Account to pay my bills.	
A piece of needed equipment goes down and requires repair or a new purchase. I am okay with using the Profit or Tax Account money for this purpose.	
I am taking a vacation and need a little extra cash to make it happen. I'm willing to "borrow" from the Profit or Tax Account for this purpose.	
I'm adding a new, high-level procedure to my offerings and I need some special equipment to fully implement the protocol. I'm fine with using money from my Profit or Tax Account for this purpose.	
Add up your score! Total:	

If you rated yourself a 6 or above on any of these statements, please go to the second bank and open your two No-temptation Accounts. It's obvious that you need them!

Self-Assessment

6

TAKING CARE OF BUSINESS: ASSESSING YOUR OWN PRACTICE

One of my favorite songs by Bachman-Turner Overdrive is "Takin' Care of Business," and it goes like this:

You get up every morning from your alarm clock's warning

Take the 8:15 into the city...

If you ever get annoyed, look at me I'm self-employed

I love to work at nothing all day

And I'll be taking care of business (every day)...[3]

Clearly, you are singing in your head right now!

Reading the lyrics to this song makes me chuckle now that I know what being self-employed looks like. If you're like me, being self-employed feels like the work never ends. And yes, being self-employed does mean you must take care of business.

When you take care of business, you set your business up to work for you—not you for it.

When you take care of business, you really do get that freedom you desire.

---

[3] Randy Bachman, "Takin' Care of Business," 1973, performed by Bachman-Turner Overdrive on *Bachman-Turner Overdrive II* (Chicago: Mercury Records), 1973, LP, track 8

When you take care of business, you know your numbers. You know where you stand. You know your profit. You have peace of mind.

So how do you take care of business? Glad you asked.

THE PROFIT FIRST FOR DENTISTS SELF-ASSESSMENT

Now that you know the core principles of Profit First, it's time to find out how you too can make it work in your business. Remember, all the money will flow into the **Income** Account and then, once a week, you will allocate by percentage to the other four core accounts; **Profit, Owner's Compensation, Tax,** and **Operating Expenses.** If you are using the No-temptation accounts, you'll then move money from your **Profit** and **Tax** accounts at your primary bank to your **Profit** and **Tax** accounts at your secondary bank.

- But how do you know what percentage you should allocate?
- How will you make sure you have enough in the **Operating Expenses** Account to pay all the bills?
- What if your current situation is really out of whack compared to what you should be doing?

These are all great questions! And you may be thinking of more.

I'm going to walk you through the process, along with the steps to do your own assessment of your dental practice business. This is one of those "gotta stick with it" activities. If you find it mind-boggling or confusing, you are not alone. This is why some dentists choose to ask for help. Either way is fine because, first and foremost, we want you to be successful. We know that this is the key piece to getting it right and making Profit First work for you.

PREPARING FOR YOUR SELF-ASSESSMENT

Step 1: *Gather all the data you're going to need to complete this assessment. Here's a checklist for you.*

☐ Profit and loss statement for the immediate last calendar year (January–December)

☐ Balance sheet for that same time period (as of December 31 of the immediate last calendar year)

☐ Tax returns for the same year

☐ Payroll reports for the same year

☐ Loan statements for the same year

☐ Credit card statements for the same year

Step 2: *Time to do some math.*

- Add up all the loan payments made in the calendar year you are using. Write down the total.

Step 3: *Gather your credit card statements.*

- Check to make sure all of the credit card charges were entered (in QuickBooks or some other accounting software) using the correct account.

- Check to make sure the credit cards have been rec-
onciled each month (just like the bank accounts).

Step 4: *Obtain your payroll report.*
- Are you, the owner-dentist, paid via payroll? If
yes, separate your payroll from the team payroll.
- Write down your net pay for the time period.
Net pay is what you took home plus any benefits
withheld from your check except taxes.
- Write down the total taxes withheld from your
payroll checks for the time period.
- Write down the total company-paid taxes just for
your owner-dentist payroll for the time period.

Step 5: *Check all records for owner draws and other
tax deposits.*
- Did you take any member draws or distributions
from the company during the time period? If
yes, write down the total.
- Did you pay any quarterly tax estimates to the
government during the time period? If yes, write
down the total.
- Did you pay any additional taxes when you filed
your return? If yes, write down the total.

By completing this assessment, you are opening yourself
to the truth about your finances. This can sometimes be a bit
stressful, especially if you know there are problems evidenced

by money struggles. All we're going to do here is take a look at how much cash came into your business and how much cash went out, along with where it went and for what purpose. Money in and money out. Super simple! If you haven't yet gathered the data in Steps 1 through 5 above, stop now and go do that first.

Okay, are you ready? No turning back now. You must do this!

Figure 6.1 is the form you will use for the Profit First for Dentists Self-assessment. If you'd like a downloadable copy of this form so you can print it and fill in the blanks, go to https://www.profitfirstdentist.com and click on the resources tab.

The first number to enter is the **real revenue**. Just so there's no confusion, here's a quick lesson on this number and some of the terms you may run across.

- **Gross Production:** Total production for the time period prior to any adjustments or write-offs.
- **Net Production:** Total production for the time period after all adjustments or write-offs. This the total collectible amount.
- **Gross Collection:** Total collected and deposited for the time period.
- **Net Collection:** Total collected for the time period, less any refunds (collection adjustments). **This number is the true real revenue.**

In the original *Profit First* book, Mike Michalowicz talks about "top line revenue" and "real revenue."[4] In case you've read

---

[4] Michalowicz, *Profit First*

his book (or not) and are wondering about these terms and what they mean, here are some definitions to help you.

Top line revenue is the total revenue or money that came into your business before payments to a subcontractor, or payments for materials that are regularly more than 20% of this total revenue. (Neither of these situations will occur in a dental practice, so you really don't need to worry about top line revenue)

Real revenue is the total revenue or money that came into your business less any refunds you made to a patient or insurance company. It's the total amount collected and deposited to your bank account less any refunds.

Follow each step in the directions for each cell.

SELF-ASSESSMENT HOW-TO

FIGURE 6.1: PROFIT FIRST FOR DENTISTS SELF-ASSESSMENT

	Actual Dollars	CAPs	PF Dentist TAPs	PF Dentist Dollars	Compare	Fix
Real Revenue	A1	100%	100%	D1	E1	F1
Profit	A2	B2	C2	D2	E2	F2
Owner's Compensation	A3	B3	C3	D3	E3	F3
Tax	A4	B4	C4	D4	E4	F4
Operating Expenses	A5	B5	C5	D5	E5	F5

A1: In the Actual Dollars column in cell **A1**, enter your total collections (**real revenue**) for the twelve-month calendar year you are using. This is your total income from your profit and loss report. In dentistry, you will not have any subcontractors or high materials costs, so there is no need to examine the difference between top line revenue and real revenue. Associate doctors and hygienists are an expense in your business no matter how you have set up their pay structure.

A2: Enter the total dollar amount deposited into a business savings account for the purpose of profit for the twelve-month calendar year. This is the cumulative profit you have sitting in the bank, or that you have distributed to yourself as a bonus on top of—but not to supplement—your salary. If you do not have profit sitting in the bank in a savings account, this means you don't really have profit.

A3: Enter the total of your net salary, plus any member draws or distributions you used personally, plus any personal expenses paid by the business for the twelve-month calendar year. This information will be available from Steps 4 and 5 in the "Preparing for Your Self-assessment" section above. Personal expenses paid by the business will be found on the profit and loss report. The

number you enter in this cell is the total benefit you received as the owner of the business and
does not include taxes.

A4: Enter the total tax your company paid on your
behalf for the twelve-month calendar year. This
number includes all taxes withheld from your
payroll, all company matching taxes, and all corporate taxes. If your company structure is such
that you take draws from the company for your
personal income, only report the total amount of
taxes the company actually paid on your behalf. If
you were scrambling at the end of the year to pay
your taxes from your personal income, do not include this amount unless you took an additional
draw from the company specifically to pay your
personal income tax.

A5: Enter the total expenses your business paid for
the twelve-month calendar year you are using.
This includes everything you paid out except
profit, owner's compensation, and taxes. Your expenses will be listed on your profit and loss report
(sometimes called an income statement). Also
be sure to add in the total of all loan payments
made for the year, since this will not show up on
the profit and loss statement. If you see something called amortization or depreciation, do not

include these items because they are considered non-cash. Remember, we are using only cash in and cash out.

B2–B5: These cells will show you your Current Allocation Percentages (CAPs). Even though you haven't been allocating money every week just yet, we've now organized your money into these four categories so we can see where you currently stand. It's now time to do the math and calculate the percentages:

> Divide A2 by A1. Multiply the answer by 100.
> Enter the result (as %) in B2.
> Divide A3 by A1. Multiply the answer by 100.
> Enter the result (as %) in B3.
> Divide A4 by A1. Multiply the answer by 100.
> Enter the result (as %) in B4.
> Divide A5 by A1. Multiply the answer by 100.
> Enter the result (as %) in B5.

C2–C5: Enter the Profit First for Dentists percentages in the Target Allocation Percentages (TAPs) column. Use Figure 6.2 below and enter the percentage in the Average column. These are the average numbers I have compiled since I began implementing Profit First with Dentists across the United States. It is worthwhile to note that I work with single owner-dentists or two-dentist partnerships with one or two locations only. These percentages may not be reflective of large group practices. I also included the range for each category so you can see that there are wide differences between practices. This is due to many factors, the most prominent being the level of Preferred Provider Organization (PPO) involvement, the number of employees in the practice, debt load, and the skill level of the dentist.

Your target could be anywhere in the Range column numbers. Refer to your CAPs to determine where you are now. Then think about where you want to go. How much and by what percentage do you want to change? Remember, this is not where you start but where you want to end up. It's also important to be realistic, because unrealistic goals kill motivation. The average is provided for information and as a guide. It is not there as a tool for you to judge yourself. We all start somewhere. The point is that we start!

If you have already busted through the average given here, good for you! What's your next level? Don't let my findings of averages hold you back. I believe that every dental practice owner who believes they can do better will benefit from the Profit First model. If you are satisfied with your profit and believe your business is as profitable as

possible already, then don't do anything different. Keep doing what you're doing. But if you're
like all the other dentists I speak with who know
they can do better, who feel the struggle every
day, then this model is for you. I know it works for
dentists because I see it working for my clients as
I guide them through the setup and implementation process.

FIGURE 6.2: U.S. DENTAL PRACTICE RANGE & AVERAGE		
Real Revenue Range of $3M and Under	Range	Average %
Real Revenue	100%	100%
Profit	1-20%	6%
Owner's Compensation	12-25%	17%
Tax	7-15%	10%
Operating Expenses	55-75%	67%

D1–D5: We'll complete some more math equations
for this row. Have your calculator ready. Using the
TAPs column percentages, we'll figure out the dollar amount for each category using your current
real revenue.

D1 = Your real revenue.

For now, use the same number you entered in **A1**. Simply copy the number from **A1** to **D1**.

Next, multiply the real revenue number in **D1** by the TAP for each row and write down this number in dollars.

D1 multiplied by **C2** = **D2**.

Enter as a total dollar amount for each item in this row.

D1 multiplied by **C3** = **D3**

D1 multiplied by **C4** = **D4**

D1 multiplied by **C5** = **D5**

These are your target Profit First for Dentists dollar amounts. Sometimes this is painful or stressful to see. Welcome to the wake-up call! I hope these numbers get you a little bit excited for change.

Remember, you are using an average percentage. You may need to adjust your own TAPs depending on where you fall in the ranges given. You may also want to try using a higher real revenue number based on the projected growth percentage you anticipate for the coming year.

E1–E5: Column **E** is the COMPARE column. This shows the difference between the current dollar amount and the target dollar amount. Take your actual dollar amount in column **A** and subtract your target amount in column **D**. You'll likely have some negative numbers. Write down the number in column **E**. A negative number means this category is experiencing a loss that you'll need to make up. For example, if you've never had a **Profit** Account or saved money in a business account before, you'll see a negative number in profit. This is the amount you'll need to make up for this account. Most likely, not all accounts will show a negative number. It's typical for the Operating Expenses Account to have a positive number. This represents the excess being spent in this category. The comparison number will show you how much you need to cut from this category. Here are the formulas to do the math:

A1 minus **D1** = **E1**

A2 minus **D2** = **E2**

A3 minus **D3** = **E3**

A4 minus **D4** = **E4**

A5 minus **D5** = **E5**

F1–F5: This is the FIX column, and you will write in the word INCREASE or DECREASE based on which direction the dollar amount needs to adjust.

For example, if your Profit in **A1** is $0 and your Profit in **D1** is $20,000, your comparison is a negative $20,000 and needs to INCREASE. Write the word INCREASE in the F column in the Profit row.

If the number in the COMPARE column is a positive number, you'll use the word DECREASE in the
FIX column.

See Figure 6.3 for an example of a completed
Self-assessment.

FIGURE 6.3: SAMPLE COMPLETED SELF-ASSESSMENT

	Actual Dollars	CAPs	PF Dentist %	PF Dentist Dollars	Compare	Fix
Real Revenue	A1 $1,200,000	B1 100%	C1 100%	D1 $1,200,000	E1 $0	F1 None
Profit	A2 $0	B2 0%	C2 6%	D2 $72,000	E2 ($72,000)	F2 Increase
Owner's Compensation	A3 $192,000	B3 16%	C3 17%	D3 $204,000	E3 ($12,000)	F3 Increase
Tax	A4 $84,000	B4 7%	C4 10%	D4 $120,000	E4 ($36,000)	F4 Increase
Operating Expenses	A5 $924,000	B5 77%	C5 67%	D5 $804,000	E5 $120,000	F5 Decrease

These numbers are quite typical of many dental practices.
The high overhead, or operating expense, is keeping this dentist
from realizing the true benefits of practice ownership. It's obvious what needs to happen in this business. Operating expenses
must be scrutinized for any over-expenditure, and that money
directed to the other three accounts. Remember, this will happen over time with a plan in place.

This assessment brings instant clarity to the business owner and can feel embarrassing at first. Embarrassment leads to hiding. Hiding the problem is what got the dentist to this point. It's now time to embrace the clarity and start taking the steps needed to improve the health of the business.

It's time to stop thinking that more production will solve the problem. Profit is not an event. It's a habit, built week by week over time. Slow and steady wins the race.

IT'S YOUR TURN: ACTION TIME!

If you've read this far and have not yet completed your own assessment, STOP now! Put this book down. Go to Appendix 1 in this book for a blank copy of the Profit First for Dentists Self-assessment form. Gather your data and complete the assessment. You need to do this if you want to move forward with Profit First in your business.

Do not let embarrassment or procrastination get in the way of this step! Get serious. Get with it. Get going!

7

Making It
All Work

7

LEARNING TAKES SOME TIME

I remember dental hygiene school and how painfully long it took to finally see my first real live patient in the clinic. The appointment was four hours long and I never even got to start the prophy. Geez! The patient had to come back for another four-hour appointment to finish. I am so grateful for those family members who believed in me and put up with those long appointments to help me learn.

I'm sure it must have been the same in dental school. Remember how much time you spent in the lab practicing on typodonts? And if we're honest here, that didn't really prepare you for all the human stuff like saliva, gag reflexes, and cheek muscles that could lift a hundred pounds. The clinic is where it all happened.

But none of us jumped right into working in the clinic on the first day. We had a lot to learn before we could be trusted with a patient. There was a learning process that started with books, diagrams, pictures, science, and lots of quizzes and exams. We then progressed to the lab and finally to the clinic. Each step built on the one that came before.

None of us went from A to Z overnight (or at least, I didn't). There were challenges. There were failures. There were celebrations. We were molded and shaped into the professionals we are today. Our beliefs were challenged. We learned new concepts. We learned to question things. We learned to get to the root cause of problems.

It's no different with Profit First and your money. Give yourself some grace when you first start out. There's no quiz or exam to pass. This is not a go big or go home kind of proposition. In fact, trying to do too much all at once will put your finances over the edge and likely you'll quit and go back to your old way of doing things. And how's that working for you?

I trust you've read this far because you're serious about Profit First and you want to make sure you do it correctly for a dental practice. Drew and I want you to be successful as well. We know how powerful this method is. We know it works.

CAPS TO TAPS

Just like dentistry, Profit First has its own jargon. These acronyms are important to understand.

- CAPs: Current allocation percentages. This is where your business is today.
- TAPs: Target allocation percentages. This is where you want your business to be in the future.

In Chapter 6, you completed your own assessment (hopefully you have this done). If you didn't do this step or you're stuck trying to do it and need help, please reach out. Send a message to Barb@BarbStackhouse.com.

Once you have your own assessment completed, with your CAPs and TAPs, you'll need to create a plan for how you'll implement the changes over time. Remember, we didn't start seeing patients on the first day of dental school. Likewise, you're not going to start with the TAPs. However, you do have to start somewhere.

Perhaps your CAP for Profit has been 0% in the past. You may decide your TAP for Profit is 10%, but you don't start out next week using the 10% allocation for Profit. That's a recipe for disaster and you'll end up robbing the **Profit** Account to pay the bills. Then you will feel like a failure and quit. Please don't do this!

The best way to move from point A to point B in the Profit First model is to start with baby steps and go slow. If you need two or three quarters to make the first changes, so be it. No one is going to judge you—except maybe yourself. And that is just chatter in your head. The committee up there doesn't know what it's talking about. Seriously, though, any movement you make in the right direction to get your business more profitable is a win. You have to stick with the plan.

CREATING THE PLAN

It's time now to get real with the numbers in your practice finances. You've already faced your CAPs. This means you are face to face with your own financial reality. How does it feel? If your percentages are close to or less than the averages

I shared, you may be feeling pretty good at this point. But if your percentages are woefully over the averages, you might be stressing a bit.

At first, you may think there's no way you can do this. Remember the committee that chatters in your head? Remember all the stories from Chapter 1 that we tell ourselves? They're all just made-up stories. Every time you feel the stress coming on, remember: THEY ARE ALL JUST MADE-UP STORIES. Yes, they feel pretty real and raw right now, but until you change the story in your head, you'll keep on believing it. And that is what got you to where you are now.

Ask yourself: Could you change things by just a few percentage points in each category? Why, yes, of course you can. That's your starting point. Figure 7.1 is a chart where you can plot out your plan. Figure 7.2 shows a completed example. The TAPs and CAPs I used are the same percentages from the example given in Chapter 6.

Create your own plan and map it out over the next four to six quarters. This gives you a year to a year and a half to work on it. If it takes you longer than that, no problem. At least you're still moving in the right direction.

FIGURE 7.1					
Category	Current %	QTR 1 Target%	QTR 2 Target%	QTR 3 Target%	QTR 4 Target%
Real Revenue					
Profit					
Owner's Compensation					
Tax					
Operating Expenses					

FIGURE 7.2					
Category	Current %	QTR 1 Target%	QTR 2 Target%	QTR 3 Target%	QTR 4 Target%
Real Revenue	100%	100%	100%	100%	100%
Profit	0%	2%	3%	4%	6%
Owner's Compensation	16%	16%	17%	17%	17%
Tax	7%	8%	9%	9%	10%
Operating Expenses	77%	74%	71%	70%	67%

TRIM THE OVERHEAD

I've never yet worked with a practice that didn't find places to cut expenses. I routinely do this for my own business as well. It's so easy to get sucked into recurring fees for things you no longer use or need. If you want to be successful with Profit First, plan on reviewing your expenses in detail. Drew and I both help our clients do this when we see that their expenses are higher than usual. Set aside some time for it. You'll be amazed at what you uncover. It's totally worth doing.

We're going to divide the overhead, or operating expenses, into two main categories. They are "fixed expenses" and "variable expenses." There will be subcategories within these two main categories, but we'll keep it all super simple here. Once you break down the expenses into the fixed or variable categories, it's much easier to see where you can start reducing expenses.

A fixed expense is one that typically remains at the same, or nearly the same, dollar amount every month. When the monthly collection increases, the fixed expense percentage goes down. When the monthly collection decreases, the fixed expense percentage goes up. Here's an example for you.

Super Dental Practice has fixed expenses of $45,000 each month.

Month 1 collection is $120,000. The fixed expense percentage for Month 1 = 37.5%

Month 2 collection is $92,000. The fixed expense percentage for Month 2 = 48.9%

The fixed expense dollar amount stayed the same; however, the revenue fluctuated, which then impacted the percentage.

A variable expense is one that typically fluctuates or changes right along with the changes in collection from month to month. It is likely that the percentage for variable expenses will remain consistent. And it makes sense that if you produce and collect more, your supply and lab costs will also increase. There will also be other expenses, like merchant fees, that go up as well. You may well spend more on marketing, too.

If Super Dental Practice usually operates at a variable expense percentage of 25%, then they could expect the following.

Month 1 collection is $120,000. The variable expenses at 25% would be $30,000.

Month 2 collection is $92,000. The variable expenses at 25% would be $23,000.

The variable expense percentage stayed the same; however, the revenue fluctuated, which then impacted the dollar amount. **The easiest place to begin trimming expenses is in the variable expense category.** Because the dollar amount fluctuates from month to month, you have greater control over these variable expenses.

Fixed expenses include the following operating expenses:

- Team compensation
- Occupancy
- Equipment and debt payments

Variable expenses include the following operating expenses:

- Dental supplies
- Lab
- Marketing
- Business administration and other

As a general rule for a dental practice, the fixed expenses should not exceed 40%. Ideally, you want them to be about 35% of revenue if at all possible. If the percentage is way over in this category, start by looking at revenue.

Ask yourself these questions:

- Is the schedule fully booked?
- Does the day fall apart at the last minute?
- Do I have enough active patients to support the amount of time available?

If you are unable to make changes to increase revenue in a timely manner, you may need to look at ways to reduce your fixed expenses. It's a bit more of a challenge, but it can be done.

As for variable expenses, the general rule is not to exceed 30% and ideally keep it to 25% of revenue or less. Scrutinize every expense and ask yourself these questions:

- Is this expense necessary to deliver quality dentistry?
- Does this expense benefit our patients and our team?
- Does this expense directly contribute to our services?
- Is this expense necessary to keep the doors open?

I think you get the idea here. Nothing is sacred. Question every expense and reduce it where possible or eliminate it altogether.

Keep in mind that these suggested percentages include all cash that went out of the office to pay any expense or loan payment in any given month. You will not find these totals or percentages on your profit and loss report. And this is why it always seems like something is missing from that report—because it is!

What I'm sharing is a very simple description, and there is certainly more to a practice or business financial picture than this. However, I've provided a great, simple foundation to operate from. The **Operating Expenses** Account will be used to pay all of these fixed and variable expenses. If you are overspending somewhere, the account will be screaming at you with low funds available.

Most of the clients that come to me for help do not know their true operating expense (overhead) percentage, let alone the breakdown between fixed and variable expenses. I can only guess that this is because they are used to looking at a profit and loss report or income statement rather than a report of all the revenue (cash in) less all the bills paid, expenses, loan payments, etc. (cash out) as a dollar amount and a percentage. Even clients I have worked with prior to finding Profit First who then converted over to the Profit First system thought they knew their overhead percentage. However, when I completed their Profit First Self-assessment and Rollout Plan, they were surprised. The numbers don't lie.

What really excites me is to see dentists who are committed to getting their business financially healthy using Profit First and making the decision to get their overhead down. It pays off in big ways, especially when it comes time for profit distributions.

Something else to consider is efficiency and investing in team training. Creating and implementing systems will also positively impact profitability. Time is money in a dental practice. Being efficient and reducing time-wasters is always a good thing. For the purposes of this book, my focus is on the actual expenses and how to reduce them; but it's good to recognize that there are other factors. Your team is your greatest asset. Invest in them!

WEEKLY RHYTHM

With Profit First for Dentists, we've found that a weekly rhythm works much better than a twice-monthly one. There are a lot of moving parts in a dental practice, and things can change quickly, so having the weekly allocations seems to work much better.

Every day, the practice collections are deposited in the **Income** Account. These deposits sit in this account and accumulate until the end of the week.

Once the week is closed out and the money has hit the bank, figure out the allocation amount based on the percentage you determined. This is where you need to be clear on your plan and your percentages. Also, remember that the order in which you transfer money from the **Income** Account to the other four core accounts does matter. Profit first, always!

Let's look at an example. I will use the percentages for QTR 1 from Figure 7.2.

> Weekly total collected and deposited in the
> Income Account = $25,000

Compute the allocations.

> Profit 2% = $500
> Owner's Compensation 16% = $4,000
> Tax 8% = $2,000
> Operating Expenses 74% = $18,500

Next, log into your online banking and transfer these amounts from the **Income** Account to each respective account. That's it! This completes the week and the cycle begins again. Use the money in the **Operating Expenses** Account to pay all your overhead expenses. Use the money in the **Owner's Compensation** Account to pay yourself. Use the **Tax** Account to pay the owner's payroll income tax. At the end of each quarter, use the **Tax** Account to pay the quarterly estimated income tax deposits when due. Otherwise, leave the money in the **Tax** and **Profit** accounts to grow. If you find there is extra in the **Tax** Account at the end of the year (and all the taxes are paid), simply transfer the excess money in the **Tax** Account to the **Profit** Account. I tell you, getting a tax bonus is a pretty sweet deal.

QUARTERLY CELEBRATION!

At the end of each quarter, it's celebration time! This is when you take your profit distribution. Remember, it's your reward for taking the risk to be a business owner. It's your pay for all the other business things you do. Calculate your profit distribution at 50% of the total deposits into the **Profit** Account for the quarter. Leave the remainder in the account to build up and provide you with a "rainy day" fund. When cash reserves build up over time in this account, you will find a certain relief of stress and peace of mind.

Resist the urge to not take your profit distribution. Yes, some dentists decide they will just leave the money in the **Profit** Account and let it accumulate faster. But wait a minute! You deserve the profit distribution. You deserve the reward. When you decide to not take your profit distribution, you are telling yourself that you're not important. I have to disagree. You are very important to this dental practice business. So go ahead and show yourself a little love. Take that profit distribution and celebrate, big time!!

Dr. Nick from upstate New York followed the rules and took his 50% profit distribution from the **Profit** Account. After just two quarters—that's two profit checks—he took his family on a weeklong vacation. How cool is that? Don't underestimate how fast the **Profit** Account will grow. As you increase the percentage of allocation each quarter, it will accumulate even faster. I get excited when it's time to take my profit distribution—yes, I use Profit First in my business, too.

CHECKLIST TO GET STARTED

Here we are the end of this chapter and, as you might be guessing, we have some action steps to take. Drew and I put together this Profit First for Dentists checklist. We like that you're reading our book, but what really gets us jazzed is you putting the principles into action. Here's a getting started checklist! No excuses, only ACTION!

Getting Started Checklist

1. Tell your bookkeeper and accountant what you're doing.
2. Get your bookkeeper and accountant on board. (If you have trouble here, go to Chapter 2, where we talk more about this.)
3. Set up your bank accounts: Open **Income**, **Profit**, **Owner's Compensation**, Tax, and **Operating Expenses** Accounts at your primary bank and secondary **Profit** and **Tax** Accounts at the no-temptation bank across town. (Seriously, if you haven't done this yet, get YO BUTT to the bank!)
4. Complete the Self-assessment and calculate your CAPs and TAPs.
5. Map out your plan for each quarter.
6. Make your allocations and transfer money each week.
7. Do everything possible to cut expenses.
8. At the end of each quarter, take your profit distribution.
9. At the end of each quarter, adjust your percentages to reach your TAPs.
10. At the end of the year, CELEBRATE your new habit of Profit First!

8

Manage Debt and Plan for the Future

8

PERSONAL AND BUSINESS DEBT

If you own your practice, chances are you've experienced having debt along the way. Dentistry is an expensive profession. There are a lot of overhead expenses necessary to run a practice and a lot of equipment required to do dentistry. Many dentists I speak with feel the weight of debt and dream of the day when it will all be paid off.

It's good to understand both personal and business debt. They both impact the practice. Your personal lifestyle affects what you do in the practice and how the business will support you. It's critical to make good decisions both personally and professionally when it comes to debt. If you have multiple loans for different things, it's a good idea to first take stock of the situation. Make a list of all your personal debt and all business debt. Here's a sample list to get you started. You will need to include the amount of debt for each category and then add up these numbers for a total.

Personal debt:
- School debt
- Home loan
- Automobile loans

119

- Second home loan
- Credit card debt (not paid off every month)
- Family loan
- Other debt

Business debt:
- Practice build-out and/or practice purchase loan(s)
- Equipment loan(s)
- Line of credit
- Credit card debt (not paid off every month)
- Family loan
- Mortgage on facility (you own your building)
- Other debt

GOOD VS. BAD DEBT

Okay, now that you have a total for both personal and business debt, it's time to understand the concept of "good" debt vs. "bad" debt.

As you might already know or speculate, credit card debt is bad debt. Why? Glad you asked. Credit card debt is usually debt you have because you couldn't pay your regular bills, and it typically carries a high interest rate. Both of these factors are reason enough to classify it as bad debt. If you can't pay your regular bills and expenses, you are overspending. Using a credit card with a high interest rate means you are overspending further.

When I talk about credit card debt, I'm referring to a balance you do not pay off at the end of each credit card's monthly cycle, which means that you or your business are being charged interest. If you have an interest charge on your credit card statement, you did not pay the balance in full. This is bad debt.

However, if you use your credit card because you want the "points" or "cash back" and you pay it off every month without fail, this is not considered bad debt. Neither is it considered good debt. When you use a credit card, it's easy to overspend. You must be disciplined and have a good tracking system in place if you choose to use a credit card to pay your bills.

If the debt incurred increases your revenue and does not create a monthly burden to you or your business, then it could be considered good debt. Typically, good debt includes debts like a mortgage for your home or office and most business loans (if they are used for generating income or to increase the value of your practice).

Bad debt, then, includes loans for items that depreciate in value, like auto loans and credit card debt. Also, if you use a loan to purchase equipment and then don't use the equipment enough to create a profit center, consider it bad debt. This goes back to the temptation to purchase at the CE course because it's the best deal right then and there. If you don't have a solid plan in place or systems to train your team, these purchases can easily become a burden. The skill you learned along with the equipment you purchased sits "on the shelf," doing nothing.

Bad debt could also be good debt in disguise. If you overbuild or purchase real estate beyond your means of repayment, you may end up in a month-to-month or week-to-week survival trap. The debt holds you hostage and feels crushing. Even though the original intention was good, the debt might be too much for your practice or personal budget to sustain. It's easy to get sucked into the "go big" model before you're ready or know what you're doing.

Personally, I believe it's best to live below your means. If you have an off month at the practice, it won't wreck your home budget and you won't be so stressed about it. The same is true of practice debt. Don't get so strapped down by debt that you are constantly working harder to meet all the demands on your business finances.

PLEASE DON'T BEAT YOURSELF UP

If you are already in debt, please do not judge yourself. Remember, this chapter began by stating the fact that almost all dentists have had debt at one time or another—or still do.

Rather than shame yourself or feel guilty about debt, it might help to understand a bit of psychology behind it. We all are influenced by internal and external forces, especially when it comes to money and debt. Robert Cialdini, Ph.D., in his book *Influence: The Psychology of Persuasion*, shares his research findings on human behavior and persuasion. He discusses six main principles of persuasion in the book[5], but I will talk about only a few of them here that I believe apply to overspending and debt in a dental practice business.

In my opinion, social proof might be the strongest psychological influencer when it comes to equipment loans in a dental

---

[5] Robert Cialdini, Ph.D., *Influence: The Psychology of Persuasion* (New York, NY: William Morrow and Company Inc., 1993)

practice. According to Cialdini, social proof in its simplest form is peer pressure. After attending a dental meeting where you've seen all the new equipment and talked to other dentists who have already adopted the new technology, you begin to think you need to keep up, too and that you'll somehow lose out if you don't adopt the newest technology or material or system. This peer pressure keeps nagging at your subconscious mind until you bite the bullet and make the purchase.

Another concept in the book *Influence*, and right up there with social proof, is the concept of authority as a psychological influencer. Simply put, people tend to follow an authority figure. When we see the leaders in dentistry adopting a new technology, we feel a stronger urge to adopt the same for ourselves. If you see your mentor using a new technology, chances are you'll want to learn more about it and will be more prone to adopt it in your own practice.

Lastly, I'll mention the idea of scarcity, also from Cialdini's research. When we are confronted with a "limited time offer," our brains automatically start working to figure out a way to take advantage of the offer. This is what trips us up at the CE course with all the equipment priced at a significantly reduced fee if purchased today. The scarcity tactic actually uses a different part of the brain and causes people to abandon the idea of working through all the pros and cons. It's as if the brain skips to a mental shortcut in making a decision.

With a little understanding of these psychological influencers, it's possible to overcome the urge to purchase now. It's possible to weigh the decision against your current cash flow. It's possible to rewire your brain. It's possible to make the purchase while being well informed and having a solid plan of action in place. The point here is to understand that not all purchases are wise decisions and that, if you want to avoid a bad purchase decision, you must first understand your current debt load along with your current cash flow picture.

GETTING OUT OF DEBT

Once you clearly understand your debt, you might be wondering how you can pay it off sooner rather than later. I'm all for paying off debt, but not at the expense of a **Profit** Account. I've watched dentists plow all their extra cash into debt payoff only to find themselves in a low-production month six months down the road and borrowing more money to pay the bills. And yes, they borrow with credit cards. So they end up in a cycle that just never seems to end.

With any plan to pay down debt, there must also be a plan to set aside profit first. In fact, the Profit First system works great for decreasing debt load. More on that in just a minute.

First, you must put a freeze on debt! No more DEBT! You must not acquire any new loans, no matter what. This is a commitment you make to yourself and your business. It seems so simple, but sticking to it can be difficult. If your go-to plan when you need to get out of a pinch with your finances is to get a loan or use a credit card, this step may be harder for you. You owe it to yourself to do this.

You must shift your thinking to a mindset of saving money, no matter what. Saving money means cash in the bank. It's been proven that a slow, methodical practice of saving a little bit each week actually works. You build the habit of saving. Setting aside your profit first easily creates this habit. Even though you have debt, you still need to save money. The point is, you build a new habit and strengthen your resolve with the debt freeze.

Once you implement the debt freeze and commit to taking your profit first, your next step is to cut costs anywhere possible. This does not mean slashing salaries or firing team members, unless you truly are overstaffed (as would be evidenced by a lack of work for them to do). If team members have to work at being busy, it might be time to assess your labor costs.

Go through your bank statement and look for the fat to trim. Keep what is necessary and let go of the things that are not generating or supporting increased income. I want you to look at everything. Nothing is sacred. Really, question every dollar you spend.

Once your **Profit** Account has built up over a quarter time period, you'll calculate your profit distribution. As the owner, you will typically take 50% of the profit deposits as a distribution; however, if you are actively working to pay down debt, this percentage may change. You may choose to take a smaller profit distribution for yourself and opt to use a larger percentage to make a payment on the principal of a loan you are working to pay off. For example, you might decide to use 70 or 80% of the total of the profit deposits for a distribution and keep 10% for yourself, using the remainder to pay down debt.

I also like Dave Ramsey's approach to paying down debt. He calls it "the snowball method." Here is the method, taken directly from one of his blog posts.

Step 1: List your debts from smallest to largest regardless of interest rate.

Step 2: Make minimum payments on all your debts except the smallest.

Step 3: Pay as much as possible on your smallest debt.

Step 4: Repeat until each debt is paid in full.

Ramsey writes, "It's all about behavior modification, not math. When it all boils down, hope has more to do with this equation than math ever will.

If you start paying on the student loan first because it's the largest debt, you won't get rid of it for a while. You'll see numbers going down on the balance, but pretty soon you'll lose steam and stop paying extra. Why? Because it's taking forever to get a win! And you'll still have all your other small, annoying debts hanging around too."[6]

Use the quarterly profit distribution in your plan to pay down debt. It's an added boost and still allows you to save some money "just in case." Once you have all of the bad debt paid off, do a reset and create a plan to pay off the good debt. And one day you'll be cheering as you make the final payment on those big loans.

---

[6] Dave Ramsey, "How the Debt Snowball Method Works," *Ramsey Solutions,* February 26, 2021: https://www.ramseysolutions.com/debt/how-the-debt-snowball-method-works

STRATEGIES FOR CASH PURCHASES

Since you have a debt freeze placed on your business, you no longer have the option to borrow money to make a big purchase. Unless it's an emergency, like your compressor went out, you can never again rely on loans or credit cards to make purchases you can't afford. In this example, "can't afford" means that you don't have the cash to pay off the credit card immediately.

There will be purchases you'd like to make. For sure, you'll be tempted when you attend the CE course and want the necessary equipment to get started. Wait! Don't get sucked in. Instead, put a plan together to make it happen. Set a timeline. Set a goal. Start setting money aside in another savings account called Equipment Purchase. You can also use part of your quarterly profit distribution to build up this fund.

Meet with your tax planner to determine your upcoming annual tax liability. This is best done near the end of the calendar year. If you have a tax liability and you already have more than enough in your **Tax** Account, you may be able to use some of those allocated tax dollars to purchase equipment, thus reducing your current tax liability. This strategy must be applied with the advice and guidance of a tax advisor who knows you and your business. Remember this: The number one rule is NO MORE DEBT! You cannot make this purchase if you have to borrow money. If you can't afford it now, keep saving and one day you'll have the cash to make the purchase.

When you do have the cash in your account to make the purchase, something else happens. All of a sudden, you start to think more about your actual need for this equipment.

Psychologically, it's harder to spend the cash in your account than the credit on your card or in your loan. This is because you never really see the money when you use credit. Everything is hidden behind loan documents. It's almost like fake money. But when it's your own cold, hard-earned cash, the story is different. You see it. You feel it. And you end up making a better decision because you are informed.

Remember Dr. Cristin? Drew and I were able to work with her using tax reduction strategies and excess cash in her **Tax** Account, along with savings she had accrued, to purchase a laser. It was the first time ever she had paid cash for such a big purchase. Yes, she does still have a practice loan payment, but she doesn't have all those small equipment loan payments she once had to deal with—and she knows she doesn't want to do that again. Having cash gave her the power to make a better decision.

Never forget this: CASH in the bank = POWER to make better money decisions.

FUTURE GROWTH IN YOUR PRACTICE

You may be wondering how you will grow your practice if your main focus is funding the **Profit** Account and getting out of debt. First, let's define practice growth. What does it mean to you, the owner of the practice? There are many numbers that may be measured and attributed to business growth in a dental practice. Here's a list to get started.

- Increased production
- Increased number of active patients

- Increased collection
- Increased number of team members or providers
- Increased number of locations

You may add more to this list.

I would challenge the idea that these things actually guarantee business growth. They might lead to growth, but they do not automatically generate growth.

As we discussed earlier in this book, increased production leads to increased expenses, such as hiring more team members to handle the influx of an increased patient load, investing in more marketing to attract those patients, and higher supply and lab bills. Unless you know exactly how to control all these costs, you'll likely find them increasing more than you thought they would.

You may also argue that debt is required to expand or grow a business. In some cases, yes, debt leads to growth. However, I've worked with dentists who are extremely stressed over debt and have no idea how to get out from under it. Adding more debt would not be a good idea for them.

The one thing I do know is that the more a dentist has in cash reserves, the more likely they are to take advantage of growth opportunities. The more profitable the practice, the more value the practice has. True practice growth includes increased practice value. Any investment you make needs to produce a return on the investment.

ACTION STEPS

Here's Your To-do List

1. List all of your debts (both personal and business).

2. Label each as either "good" or "bad" debt.

3. Use the snowball method and begin paying off bad debt now.

4. Use part of your quarterly profit distribution to further pay off bad debt.

5. If you need to make a purchase, save up the cash beforehand.

Tax Strategies
for Dentists

9

HAVE A GAME PLAN

I know you're thinking it, and I'll say it: Taxes are about as exciting as performing a root canal—on yourself. But since the only things guaranteed in life are death and taxes, we need to address the latter. So, without further ado, let's get started!

Most dentists we meet do not have a game plan to minimize taxes. Based on that, the perception is that the overwhelming majority of CPAs, in a way, seem to work for the IRS. They don't work with their clients to aggressively minimize taxes. They are there to prepare forms to file for the government. Really, they work as an extension of the IRS. Don't get me wrong, I'm not saying there aren't great CPAs out there that work as tax-saving advocates for their clients—we just don't see them very often.

If minimizing taxes is a priority for you, read on. There is much to learn before making any decision about tax strategies or who you'll trust to help you. Begin with determining how aggressive you are willing to be with your deductions, and whether your CPA is willing to be that aggressive too. Later in the chapter, we will dive into some of the most obvious tax deductions dentists might miss. But for now, let's go over the most basic foundational matter: how your legal entity impacts your taxes and your journey with Profit First.

SOLE PROPRIETORSHIP

A sole proprietorship is the simplest, cheapest, and fastest way out there to do business. It works like this. You, the dentist, decide you want to open your own dental practice. So you simply start seeing patients in a space you lease, finish out, and equip, or use a practice that you purchase under your name, such as "Seymour Perio, DDS." There is no need to formally register this entity with your state and no need for any fancy footwork. You simply do business, as you.

Simplicity is a beautiful thing—at least usually—but simplicity, in this case, may or may not be the best thing for you. I'll admit I'm not an attorney, and this isn't legal advice, but one of the basic issues with a sole proprietorship is not having any legal protection from something going sideways in your practice. In fact, no legal entity will protect you from your own personal malpractice. That's what you have insurance for. However, a sole proprietorship doesn't afford you any protection in the event that a patient falls and hurts themselves, a ceiling light falls on a team member, or an associate dentist drops an endo file down a patient's throat (just to name a few examples). It seems like we've heard it all! One thing we know is that dentists, especially those who start out using a super-simple-makes-all-the-sense-in-the-world cash flow system like Profit First, are going to build assets and a net worth. Those assets and growth are worth protecting.

Let's dive into how being a sole proprietor works with Profit First and the role of the **Tax** Account. Back in Chapter 6, we discussed target allocation percentages (TAPs) and how you'll move money from your **Income** Account to each of your other four core accounts. The **Tax** Account is one of those four core accounts. As a sole proprietor, the TAP for taxes needs to include your income tax, both federal and state, and your self-employment tax. Every time you sit down to allocate the money that has accumulated in your **Income** Account, you'll transfer your TAP to your **Tax** Account and it will continue to grow throughout the year. Then, when you meet with your CPA each quarter to determine how much tax you should pay in with your estimated tax payments, you'll have a war chest of cash built up and set aside for this very specific purpose!

While a sole proprietorship is simple, that doesn't mean it's the best choice for you. Take your time, consider your options, and choose wisely.

LIMITED LIABILITY COMPANY

The most common way for a dentist to conduct business is as a limited liability company (LLC). Much like a sole proprietorship, a limited liability company can be a very simple way to conduct business. The primary difference is that the business is no longer synonymous with you personally. It's now a separate legal entity formed under the rules and regulations of your state. Unlike a sole proprietorship, the limited liability company provides you some basic legal protection for your personal assets. Consult with an attorney licensed in your state if you want to dig into the weeds further on legal protection. It can get dirty, very quick!

Conducting business as a limited liability company provides tremendous flexibility to you as a business owner. It grows with you, so to speak. Whether you're starting a new dental practice from scratch or running a multimillion-dollar, multi-location dental service organization, a limited liability company could work for you. In most cases, as your practice matures, you will eventually file an election to be treated as an S corporation for tax purposes.

If you elect not to be treated as an S corporation for tax purposes, taxation as a limited liability company operates exactly as it does for a sole proprietorship. You are subject to income tax, both federal and state, as well as self-employment tax on your profit earned by your limited liability company. Your **Tax** Account will operate the same as it does for a sole proprietorship. Each time you allocate your funds from your **Income** Account, you'll transfer your TAP allocation for taxes to your **Tax** Account, watch it grow, and then you will suck the life right back out of it with your quarterly estimated tax payment made to Uncle Sam. Good times!

Limited liability companies are not difficult to set up, nor are they difficult to maintain. The specifics of forming a limited liability company are beyond the scope of this book but I tell you the process is different, state-by-state, and encourage you to reach out to an attorney and CPA to find out how to form one in your state.

C CORPORATION

In stark contrast to the limited liability company, the C corporation is the least common way for a dentist to conduct business. The creation of a corporation is very similar to that of a limited liability company. Paperwork is filed with the Secretary of State in your state and, once approved, you may begin conducting business as a corporation.

A C corporation is the least common way to conduct business, mainly because of double taxation. A C corporation files its own tax return, but unlike other legal entity types, the corporation's profit does not flow through to the owner's personal tax return. Instead, the corporation's profit is taxed and its earnings retained. Then, if the owner wants to disperse any earnings, they must do so as a dividend. Once a dividend is disbursed, the owner pays personal income tax on the dividend, hence the double taxation. As the sum of the corporate income tax and tax on the dividends received is higher than the highest personal income tax bracket, there is no financial gain, from a tax perspective, in this arrangement. There may be other reasons to conduct business as a corporation, such as the need to provide employee benefits or retirement planning, but those reasons are beyond the scope of this book.

To sum up: 99% of the time, there is no benefit to dentists from operating as a C corporation, or reason to do so. Consult a dental CPA if you're told otherwise.

S CORPORATION

Along with establishing a limited liability company as the legal entity, most dentists file an election with the IRS to be treated as an S corporation. Conducting business as an S corporation has its tax advantages. Namely, profit earned by the business passes through to the shareholder (S). A common misconception about the S corporation is the idea that the status is a legal entity itself, to be formed through the Secretary of State. In actuality, it is an election filed with the IRS.

You can be either a limited liability company or a C corporation and file an election to request the IRS treat you as an S corporation for tax purposes. There are some unique tax rules for conducting business as an S corporation. If you're working with a good dental CPA, they will help you navigate these rules and maximize the value of having your practice taxed as an S corporation.

One of the rules that differentiates the treatment of an S corporation from that of a limited liability company taxed as a disregarded entity is the requirement of having its shareholder on payroll. Tax law requires an S corporation shareholder to be paid reasonable compensation. Determining what reasonable compensation is for you is an art rather than a science. There is no exact formula! Essentially: What would you pay someone else to perform the duties you are performing? For many of us, these duties include being a dentist—but they also involve performing human resources and banking tasks, management duties, and likely much more. Why does this matter, you ask? It matters because the higher the salary you pay yourself, the higher your payroll taxes are. Ideally, you would pay as little in salary compensation as possible in order to avoid paying payroll taxes. This is one of the biggest benefits of being treated as an S corporation for tax purposes.

The bottom line is: No matter what type of legal entity you have chosen to conduct business under, there is a way forward with Profit First.

EVERYONE LIKES TAX DEDUCTIONS

How aggressive do you want to be when it comes to tax deductions? Everyone has their own comfort level with this. It's best to find a CPA or tax strategist who aligns with your same level of risk. Here are some general rules to keep in mind when working with a CPA and filing taxes.

Always Report All Income

It's important to report all income to the IRS. This means it needs to be reported to your CPA as well. Hiding money from the government is never a good plan. In fact, underreporting income will land you in the slammer.

Take Liberties with Deductions

Since any and all deductions will help to reduce tax liability, it's important to make sure you take all deductions possible. This might be a gray area for some, and you'll need to decide your own comfort level. Look for ways to make everyday expenses legitimately tax-deductible.

Automobile Deductions

If you're willing to drive an SUV or a truck, there are some advantages in the tax code. Ideally, you can choose a 6000-lb. SUV to take advantage of section 179. Section 179 of the tax code was created for small businesses to deduct the full price of a qualified equipment purchase. Trucks with beds greater than six feet in length may also qualify. The deduction for vehicles is a bit different than equipment but is still a significant amount. A vehicle lease can also be structured to take advantage of this tax deduction. Remember, tax codes can and do change, so the deduction amount may be different from year to year. The point here is, if you are going to purchase a vehicle, it might make sense to use the tax code to your advantage.

Even if you are not making an auto purchase, you may write off depreciation and deduct other auto expenses such as repairs, fuel, insurance, maintenance, car washes, and even the little green smelly pine tree! If you choose to write off actual expenses for your auto, you will not be able to take the mileage deduction. It's one or the other. So it's important to keep records and determine which has the greater benefit.

Get serious about these auto deductions and keep a mileage log for at least ninety days in order to substantiate your greater-than-50% business use. (There are apps that help do this and make it easy-peasy.) One way to take advantage of this is to have your primary office in your home and your clinical office as your secondary office. This will greatly improve your business mileage as you travel between the two on a daily basis.

Hiring Your Children

As a business owner, you can hire your kids and pay them up to $12,000 for the year completely tax-free. There are many things they can do to earn this money. Besides emptying the trash or sweeping the floor, they can help with social media or even model for a social media post.

If you want to fund your child's future, you can take advantage of a Roth IRA contribution. Check with your CPA for the amount limitations. Funding your kids' education is also a great way to utilize tax deductions. As your children approach their college years, they can transition to becoming your marketing expert or even being listed on your board of directors, qualifying additional write-offs at a tax rate of zero.

Write Off Your Travel

When you travel for continuing education, the expenses are deductible. Many doctors tack on vacation time either prior to or after the CE event, thus making their vacation travel expenses a write-off.

It's also possible to hold a "board of directors" meeting at a specified location that just so happens to be your vacation spot. Bam! Another write-off. Remember, your college-aged kids are on the board!

Maybe you're checking out a new lab or supplier. The time and travel spent researching, networking, and developing new products or procedures, along with any additional equipment purchases, are all tax-deductible.

Home Office

In the Automobile Deductions section, we mentioned having a home office to support the mileage accumulation between your home business office and your clinical office. There are some requirements, so make sure you discuss the details with your CPA. It is possible to conduct business from a home office. Think about things like phone calls to check on patients, bookkeeping, bank transfers, logging into the patient database to complete notes, etc. Again, this is something to discuss with your CPA.

Don't Play Audit Roulette

If a possible deduction is known to cause a red flag and initiate an audit from the IRS, it may not be worth the headache or risk. It's always best to consult a professional before making a decision about any category of deductions. Again, this all comes down to your risk level and that of your CPA or tax strategist.

TAX-SAVING INVESTMENTS
Retirement Contributions

There are different types of plans available that enable small business owners to set up regular contributions to a retirement plan. This is also a way to help team members begin to think about their own futures. Many offices choose to use a 401(k) plan because it allows them to help fund the plan with profit sharing and cash balance contributions. It's best to speak with a financial planner and a tax strategist to make sure this is the best option for you and your situation.

Tax Savings Investments

By saving money on taxes, you'll have additional cash available in your business. If you invest these savings on a regular basis and use a strategy that gives a good return on the investment, you will create a nice nest egg over time. One of the simplest, easiest ways to invest is to utilize compounded interest in a savings or investment plan. If you invested just $10,000 of tax savings provided by aggressive tax deductions every year, over a thirty-year career, you'd have over a million dollars!

Other Investment Strategies

Of course, there are other types of investment strategies including real estate or other business investments. The important thing to remember is to hire a professional to help you. Have a plan and follow the plan. Know what you are doing and how to get through the challenges when they come—because they will.

FINDING THE CPA FOR YOU

Just as not all dentists are created equal, not all CPAs are created equal. There are CPAs who are willing to take more risk and others who are risk-averse. There are CPAs who specialize in a particular profession or type of business and others who serve a variety of businesses. The key is to find the one for you.

So how do you vet a good CPA for your dental practice? In Chapter 2, we discussed some questions to use to help get your CPA on board with your Profit First plan. But what if you're feeling like a change is needed after all? There is hope. The good news is that there are many CPAs who work specifically with dentists, and there are also those who, like Drew, are both Certified Profit First Professionals and specific to dentistry.

If you want a dental-specific CPA, you might begin by looking at the list of CPAs who belong to the Academy of Dental CPAs. There are over 8,000 members in the academy, trusted by dentists nationwide. Yes, Drew is a member—and in his own words, "I am biased, but you should be too!" Visit https://www.adcpa.org for more information.

10

Facing the Challenges

10

IN THEORY

You've read this far and are thinking it all sounds good. It really shouldn't be that difficult. In fact, you may be scheming to create your own, modified Profit First method.

You may be thinking that it's the theory that matters. Why would you need to open all those accounts? It should work just as well using a spreadsheet. You may think as long as you keep track of all these different categories, everything will work fine. But it doesn't.

Theory is one thing. Behavior is another. Profit First is a behavioral system. This means that you have to take action and do it the way it was designed, because the design is based on human behavior. If reports and spreadsheets worked so well, there wouldn't be a need for the Profit First system. Profit First exists because entrepreneurs need help with their finances. Profit First works because it's simple and behaviorally sound.

When you want to know how much money you have to make a purchase, you open your online banking and have a look. This behavior is consistent with most humans. It's what we do. Profit First is designed to capitalize on this common behavior around money. If you're going to open your online banking and have a look, why not use multiple accounts, each for a specific purpose? You'll know immediately how much money you have and for which purpose.

> **Challenge #1:** Thinking you can do this using a spreadsheet (and no additional bank accounts).

Please trust us on this. The bank accounts are necessary. They make Profit First so simple to understand and implement. The accounts are required, not optional.

GETTING CAUGHT UP IN THE DETAILS

The analytical, perfectionist side of being a dentist tells you to check, recheck, and check again before you dive in to do this. You can get lost in all the details, trying to make sure your allocation percentages are perfect before you take action. You could get stuck in analysis paralysis.

If you tell yourself you'll get started once you have exact allocation percentages or when you get caught up with all your "books" or whatever else your excuse may be, you are probably being too analytical. Don't let anything get in the way of your implementing Profit First.

If you happen to be number savvy anyway, trust yourself and get to it. Follow the instructions, figure out your percentages and get started. Even if you begin with 1% in the **Profit** Account each week, you'll be headed in the right direction.

Challenge #2: Thinking the numbers need to be perfect to get started.

If numbers are foreign to you and you feel lost in this process, then you may want to reach out for some assistance. Even if you fall into this category, do the 1% allocation to the **Profit** Account to begin. Yes, details are important, but they should not hold you back.

GO BIG OR GO HOME

Another common mistake is to go all-in, thinking you can begin with a 20% allocation to the **Profit** Account right out of the gate. If you haven't taken the time to work through your numbers and percentages, you're taking a big gamble.

The sad thing, is you'll eventually give up and decide Profit First doesn't work for you. Our advice is to start small and grow your profit percentage over time. Most dentists are not allocating 20% to profit, and especially not when they're just getting started.

Challenge #3: Doing too much too fast.

The key to overcoming this challenge is to follow each step in the process. Take enough time to figure out the current health of your business and the current allocation percentages. Once you know those numbers, you can set some realistic target goals and get started.

ACCOUNTABILITY

Having an accountability partner is one of the best ways to stay on track. This is true no matter what goal you are working to achieve. The commitment level goes way up when you know someone else is there to hold you accountable.

You'll need to tell someone about this if you want accountability. Otherwise, it's like kicking the tires, or dipping your toe in the water instead of taking a swim: You're not really committed. When you keep a goal to yourself, the only person you'll disappoint is yourself. Unfortunately, most of us are okay with disappointing ourselves, yet we'd never think of doing that to someone else.

Challenge #4: Thinking you can do this on your own.

Many have gone before you. Why not take advantage of their knowledge? Why not have someone to help you make the tough decisions? Why not do it correctly the first time?

Without accountability, you end up wasting time. What is your time worth?

With an accountability partner, or someone in your corner to make sure each step is correct, your success with Profit First will soar. Think about how it feels to share the weight with someone else. That someone will be there cheering you on when you want to throw in the towel.

Take my advice here and get yourself an accountability partner. If you need more than that, get yourself an experienced coach.

GROW FIRST (AND PROFIT LATER)

This challenge is within your own mind. It implies that you must choose between growth and profit. No way! Nothing could be further from the truth. That is plain nonsense!

Growth and profit go hand in hand. When your business is profitable, it will open the doors to growth. In fact, being profitable is the one thing you can do if you want to ensure growth.

Challenge #5: Thinking you won't have profit if you are in growth mode.

If someone else were to invest in your business, they'd first want to know how profitable it is. Wouldn't you want the same? I mean, really, if you are going to invest in your own business, you'd better make sure it's a good investment—producing a return called profit.

Focus on profit, and do it first, before investing in anything else to "grow" your business. The money in, money out equation must equal excess cash flow.

If you're struggling with cash flow, there are three things you can do to change the situation.

1. Reduce expenses
2. Increase revenue
3. A combination of both

It's time to go searching for the hidden profit in your practice. It's there.

CUTTING THE WRONG COSTS

By now, you're probably thinking about all the expenses your business incurs on a regular basis and how you will go about reducing those expenses. What will you cut? What will you keep? What can you reduce?

Challenge #6: Fear of making a mistake when cutting costs.

It's common to look at the list of expenses and not know where to begin. Everything appears to be important and necessary. So where do you start?

I suggest you approach this task with a new set of eyes. Ask yourself if this thing or service is absolutely needed for you to deliver the dentistry you do. See if you can find a different, less expensive vendor. Are there overlapping services that you could consolidate, or additional features of these services that you could use but may not have even known were available? Technology is expensive, and many times we don't fully utilize it. Dig in deeper and see what you have and how it can help you be more efficient.

Check the ROI of everything. Is it bringing money into the business? Is it of value? Is it saving you time or money? Invest in things that help you become more efficient. And then check to make sure it really does produce an ROI.

You must begin to enjoy saving more than you enjoy spending. Celebrate with high fives whenever you eliminate or reduce an expense. Remember, not all expenses need to or should be cut. Keep a frugal mindset and choose wisely.

"PLOWBACK" OR "REINVEST"

Mike Michalowicz says it best: "These are fancy terms to justify taking money out of our different allocation accounts to cover immediate expenses."[7] "Plowback" and "reinvest" are just different ways to say the word "borrow."

> **Challenge #7:** Thinking you can "borrow" from your bank accounts to "reinvest" in the **Operating Expenses** Account—and that you'll pay it back sometime.

When there isn't enough money in the **Operating Expenses** Account to cover expenses, it's a big RED FLAG! Your expenses are too high. You must find a way to fix it, fast. If this only happens once or twice over a long period of time, it could mean that you need to reassess and make sure your allocation percentages are correct.

However, if you find yourself using a credit card or line of credit to pay the bills because you think it will buy you some time, you're only lying to yourself. It's money you do not have. Credit cards ultimately result in debt. I know you tell yourself it's short-term debt to justify getting all your points. If you do pay off the card in full every month and you NEVER have

---

[7] Michalowicz, *Profit First*

interest fees, then I'll agree. Can we also agree, it's still debt and you're still working to pay it off every month?

When you find you have bills to pay and not enough in the **Operating Expenses** Account to pay them, stop and reassess. There is a better, more sustainable way to deal with this than raiding your other accounts and plowing money back into the business. Your business is screaming at you to do something different. Listen to it!

11

What Are You Waiting For?

11

NOW IS THE TIME

Congratulations, you've read this far and have now arrived at the last chapter of this book. Not everyone will make it here. Some will read this far and never take action. Others will take some action and then later give up on the process.

I encourage you to get started now. Do not wait. Do not think things will be better next month and then you'll start. Please don't get sucked into the "waiting for the right time" trap. Recognize that it's a trap and you can get caught there for a long time.

My true hope is that if you have read this far, you've been inspired and you have taken action. No excuses, just action and implementation. There's no better time than now to make your practice a Profit First dental practice.

SIMPLE STEPS FOR THE FIRST YEAR
Week One:

Mike Michalowicz, author of *Profit First*, says that the first thing to do is tell your accountant. You want your accountant on board and supportive of you growing your business with the

Profit First for Dentists model. We already talked about this in Chapter 2.

If you meet with negativity from your accountant, you'll have a decision to make. You can either work to educate them and get them on board—and it needs to be wholeheartedly on board...or you can opt to choose a Profit First Accountant, like the coauthor of this book, Drew. I hope you luck out with an accountant who will partner with you and be on board with Profit First from the start.

Once your accountant is on board, the next step is to set up the bank accounts. Remember, your existing bank account will be one of the five core accounts. You'll need to decide if you want it to be your **Income** Account (deposits are already set up to go there) or the **Operating Expenses** Account (there are probably some auto-pay items from this account). Don't forget the **Profit** Account, the **Tax** Account, and the **Owner's Compensation** Account. If you keep your current account and use it as the **Income** Account, you will also need to open an **Operating Expenses** (checking) Account.

Next, do the Self-assessment and settle on your current allocation percentages (CAPs) and your target allocation percentages (TAPs).

Week Two:

Make sure all your auto-pay debits are coming out of the **Operating Expenses** Account and/or that any automatic deposits are landing in the **Income** Account. Dentists, I highly recommend keeping your current checking account as your **Income**

Account if dental benefits are already automatically deposited there. The benefits are harder to change than the auto-debits.

Make a list of all auto-debits from your current account. Go through them and indicate if you can make the change by logging into an online platform or if you will need to call the business. Work your way through the list, making the changes. This can be time-consuming. If someone else can help you, that's great, but my experience is that the owner must make the change or give authorization.

Start your allocations and keep up with the weekly transfers. It's best to set a certain day of the week to do this. Put it on your calendar. Block out the time for it. It doesn't take long, but it must be completed.

Month 1:

Once you have consistently made allocations and transfers for a month, you will begin to see where your money is going. It's time to focus and decide where you can begin to cut expenses. Reread Chapter 7 for help with this process.

Pay attention to each week and each month. At the end of each month, take a look at all the cash that flowed into and out of your business.

Were you able to pay all your bills with the current allocation percentage to the **Operating Expenses** Account?

Was there any extra money left over in the **Operating Expenses** Account?

Or did you run short of money to pay all the bills in a timely manner?

Your business will begin to tell you what is going on and where you need to make changes. If this is Greek to you, reach out to us. Having a coach makes all the different in the world. You may only need a little bit of help. Why not explore the possibility?

Quarter 1:

Beginning with the first quarter's end, and every quarter thereafter, take your profit distribution. The dates for these distributions from the **Profit** Account are April 1, July 1, October 1, and January 1 every year.

The profit distribution consists of 50% of your deposits to the **Profit** Account for the quarter. The remaining 50% stays in the **Profit** Account to build up a reserve in case you have an emergency or things get really bad. I recommend that you eventually have two to three months of practice expenses reserved so you can pay the bills if something happens.

Once you have met the reserve, you can then determine what you want to do with your **Profit** Account money. Perhaps there's some equipment you'd like to purchase or upgrade. Start saving for it and pay cash when you have it. Maybe it's time to invest in your team. Hire a coach or take your team with you to some high-level CE. Make a vacation of it.

If you are working to pay off debt, by all means, use some of your Profit Distribution for this. In fact, it's okay to use more than 50% for debt reduction. For example, you could use 80% of the **Profit** Account deposits and pay down debt with 70%, leaving 10% for the owner distribution.

Another quarterly activity is to make a tax deposit with the government if you are making those quarterly estimated payments. Simply use the money accrued in your **Tax** Account and make the payment.

Lastly, every quarter, take a look at your CAPs and TAPs and make adjustments if necessary.

Year 1:

At the end of the year, do a good overall review of how you've done implementing Profit First. Assess how you did and compare it to your target percentages. Also, be sure to have a discussion with your accountant with regard to tax planning. This is super important. Do not wait until April 15 to see if you are on track with enough money in your **Tax** Account to cover the previous year's tax liability. In fact, the first quarter of the new year is when your **Tax** Account starts accruing money for the current year, not making up for last year.

CREATING THE PROFIT FIRST LIFESTYLE

What will you do with your quarterly profit distributions? Will you celebrate? Will you make a purchase? Or take a vacation?

The profit distribution gives you a taste of financial freedom. How does it feel to have profit set aside just for you and your business? Imagine the possibilities as you increase your profit allocation and decrease your expenses each quarter. Think about how it will feel to have all your debt paid off.

Financial freedom means that you do life on your terms. You choose to work because you want to. It means that you've reached a point where the money you have saved or invested now yields enough interest to support your lifestyle and continues to grow.

It may seem so far away if you're just getting started—but you need to know that you will only gain financial freedom if you do get started. It will happen because of the daily, weekly, quarterly, and yearly plan you put in place for saving money. Profit First is the perfect system for this.

Because you own a business, your personal life and business life are intertwined. One affects the other. You must keep your personal expenses under control. The more you spend personally, the more you take from your business. If your business can afford it, that's fine, but if not, you are creating real problems.

Try living below your means so you can save or invest even more. The more you set aside now, the sooner you will arrive at your own financial freedom. Ask yourself the tough questions. Get real with your personal spending habits.

Say NO to debt. Credit card debt is the worst. Use the snowball method and eliminate it all together. Then cut up the credit cards. This is a no-temptation activity! If you don't have them, you won't be tempted. Assess all your personal debt. Assess it based on your income. Make sure your income is in line with your healthy business plan. Your business funds your life, but you never want your lifestyle to hurt your business. There's a fine line to walk here.

WHAT ARE YOU WAITING FOR?

Honestly, do I need to ask? Okay, I will. What are you waiting for?

I hope that what Drew and I have shared in this book has inspired you to take action. Even if your business is doing well, Profit First can make a difference. You can do better. Profit First will make an impact on businesses of any size—there is no limit. It also works across many different types of businesses and, I would add, many different types of dental practice businesses.

If you're completely happy with the level of profit your business is generating, put down this book and walk away. You don't need it.

However, if you know your business finances need some help, step up and take action. Get Profit First going as quickly as possible. Six months or a year from now, you'll be emailing to tell me how much of a difference it's made.

We are cheering you on!!

Acknowledgments

This project began with Mike Michalowicz. Had he not written the book *Profit First*, Drew and I would not be publishing *Profit First for Dentists*. I am forever grateful for his guidance, mentorship, and genuine helpfulness in writing this book. Mike, you are one of the most generous people I know, so thank you for all you have done and continue to do.

Special mention to our copy editor, Zoë Bird, and our typesetter, Olaf Nelson, who both just know their stuff. You have both been a great asset to this project. Jim Reyland of Audio Productions–Nashville, thank you for the amazing audio version of this book. Your process and attention to detail, to produce a perfect outcome, is second to none.

I would be remiss if I didn't mention all the dental professionals who have shaped and guided me throughout my career. I love dentistry, and I love the profession of dental hygiene. From my dental hygiene instructors to the dentists I've been privileged to work with over the years, along with the practice management leaders and mentors who believed in me and encouraged me to grow beyond my own dreams, I thank you! You all know who are, and I wouldn't be where I am today without you. I certainly couldn't have written this book without all I've learned from you.

Drew Hinrichs, you know I appreciate you. But do you know how much? Honestly, I feel so incredibly blessed to know you, to call you friend, and now to be your coauthor. You are a true gem for the dental profession. Thank you for choosing me to put our collective ideas and thoughts into words.

On the personal side, my number one fan and cheerleader is my husband, Kevin. We've been married forty-two years now. Yes, we were just kids—high school sweethearts. It's difficult to put into words just how much he does for me. Most of the time it's the unspoken support, day in and day out, that consistently keeps me going. I know I'm lucky to have him. He never doubts my crazy ideas, and even likes to dance! Kevin, thank you for loving me through this season of writing like a madwoman— and all the other things it takes to write and launch a great book! I appreciate you, always!

Barb Stackhouse, RDH, M.Ed.,
Mastery Level Certified Profit First Professional

Appendix 1

THE SELF-ASSESSMENT FORM

	Actual Dollars	CAPs	PF Dentist TAPs	PF Dentist Dollars	Compare	Fix
Real Revenue	A1	100%	100%	D1	E1	F1
Profit	A2	B2	C2	D2	E2	F2
Owner's Compensation	A3	B3	C3	D3	E3	F3
Tax	A4	B4	C4	D4	E4	F4
Operating Expenses	A5	B5	C5	D5	E5	F5

Appendix 2

GLOSSARY OF KEY TERMS

CAPs (Current Allocation Percentages): These are the current percentages you use to allocate money from the **Income** Account to your "small plates," or other bank accounts, every week.

Financial Freedom: Financial freedom means you do life on your terms. You choose to work because you want to. It means you've reached a point where the money you have saved or invested now yields enough interest to support your lifestyle and continues to grow.

Fixed Expense: A fixed expense is one that typically remains at the same, or nearly the same, dollar amount every month. When the monthly collection increases, the fixed expense percentage goes down. When the monthly collection decreases, the fixed expense percentage goes up.

GAAP (Generally Accepted Accounting Principles): A set of accounting standards and procedures use by most businesses and following the basic formula of SALES – EXPENSES = PROFIT, thereby treating profit as an afterthought.

Income Account: A business checking account used to hold all the deposits of money coming into the business. You do not pay the bills from this account.

Once a week, allocate by percentage from this account to your other bank accounts.

No-temptation Accounts: These two extra accounts to hold the money for profit and taxes in a bank across town are there to protect you from yourself. They are designed to be difficult for you to access, so when or if the day comes when you run short of money in the **Operating Expenses** Account, you will have to think twice about stealing from yourself.

Operating Expenses Account: A business checking account used to receive allocations from the **Income** Account and designated for the sole purpose of paying all the bills.

Owner's Compensation Account: A checking account used for the sole purpose of holding and distributing money to pay the owner (dentist) of the business for the work they do delivering dentistry.

Parkinson's Law: C. Northcote Parkinson's adage that work expands to fill the available time is the same tendency your business has to use up all the available resources. This is also known as induced demand, and it's the reason why you need to stow away your profit before you find ways to spend it.

Profit: Profit is the money set aside before you pay your team, yourself, and all the bills. Without this additional profit, you feel like you're always chasing your tail to get ahead.

Profit Account: A business savings account used for holding profit, the money set aside to provide a cash distribution to the owner(s) of the practice at the end of every quarter. It's the reward for taking the risk and working all those additional hours to run your company.

Primacy Effect: Our tendency to place greater emphasis on what we encounter first. So, if profits are important to you, you'll put profit first.

Quarterly Profit Distribution: Once-per-quarter distribution of money from the **Profit** Account used to pay yourself (the owner) for all the risk you take and the work you do as the owner of the business.

Self-assessment: The process of using data gathered from business reports and making sense of it using the Profit First methodology, and the process used to figure out your own allocation percentages.

TAPs (Target Allocation Percentages): The ideal percentage of revenue you should eventually aim to allocate to your **Profit, Tax, Owner's Compensation,** and **Operating Expenses** Accounts.

Tax Account: A savings account used for holding and distributing money to fund the income tax of the owner(s).

Variable Expense: A variable expense is one that typically fluctuates or changes right along with the changes in collection from month to month. It is likely that the percentage for variable expenses will remain consistent.

Contact the Authors

BARBARA STACKHOUSE, RDH, M.ED.

I would love to hear from you, and hear about your story of using Profit First in your practice. If you'd like to reach out to me, here's where you can find me:

Email me: Barb@BarbStackhouse.com

Premier Profit First Program for Dentists:

https://www.profitfirstdentist.com

Business and speaker website:

https://www.moretolife.dental

Find my Profit First for Dentists business page on Facebook:

www.facebook.com/Profit-First-for-Dentists-213516312791823

There's also a private Facebook group, Profit First for Dentists (for dentists only). Here's the link to join:

https://group.profitfirstdentist.com

Check out my Profit First for Dentists YouTube channel for weekly videos:

https://youtube.profitfirstdentist.com

DREW HINRICHS, CPA
Owner of Engage Advisors:
https://engageadvisors.com

Drew's website has a "Schedule a Call" button to use if you'd like to reach out to him.